CONTENTS

FIGURES

I believe every leader, lay and ordained, in the church today is called to be a change agent. We do not have to change everything, just those things that are killing the church, the things that are keeping us from being faithful and growing witnesses in today's world.

Nobody needs to tell any North American church leader that our culture is in the midst of incredible change. The question is, How does one approach such change? One may regard it with fear and resentment, expecting the worst. Or one may welcome it, viewing this era as an exciting time to be alive and entrusted by God with the challenges of mission and ministry. If we take the first approach and focus on our fear, there is not much we can learn that will help us succeed and thrive. But if we take the latter approach and embrace this era as a "kairos" moment, an opportunity, then you have in your hands a book that will be an important tool, a road map of the wonderful and treacherous land of institutional change.

This map shows us that constructive change processes do not just "happen." Rather, they have an internal structure. If you recognize this structure and work with it, you can accomplish remarkable things. If you ignore this structure, you do so at your own peril and at the peril of your institution. Some so-called natural leaders may be able to do by instinct what is necessary, but most of us will be more effective if we take the time to reflect on our situation. If we arrogantly rush toward change without doing what is necessary to bring our people with us, it is certain there will be trouble. Effective change requires trust building.

We need to remember that many people like the current state of affairs and do not see the need for change in our faith communities. Some of these folks just have a naturally low tolerance for change and might think, "Nothing should ever be done for the first time!" Others simply have so much stress in their lives that the mere thought of change—more stress—creates resistance in them. Some people just like things the way they are and are not looking for a new and exciting mission. They are not asking what God might regard as faithfulness. They are happy with the church as it is, which is why they are there. They figure that if they wanted change, they would go somewhere else!

On the one hand, all of these reasons for resisting change have some legitimacy. After all, our world is changing at a frightening pace, and one valid function of church might be to provide us with some sense of the unchanging, the eternal, in the midst of the temporal and passing. On the other hand, God raises up leaders to keep the church moving forward. Churches are meant to be living bodies, not shrines. If we hold this view of the church, we must be prepared to meet resistance with love and caring but also with firm determination.

Even those who recognize the need for change will find it stressful. Even when we see the need for change, there is a part of our psyche that will resist it. Human beings have an innate need for ritual, for example, which by definition changes little. Ritual offers a certain kind of comfort in the face of the constant change in life. This is one reason why change in any routine, even the arrangement of the furniture in the church parlor, is resisted at some level by almost everyone. This is also the reason why changes in the worship service rank so high on the Richter scale of church change! Thinking about my own resistance to change, I recognize the need for learning new hymns and songs, for example, but I still do not like learning them. I confess that I groan inwardly when the song leader says, "Now we're going to learn a new one!" All change must be approached carefully and sensitively.

When ministers are called to a congregation, they usually go with an idea about some things they want to accomplish in the new setting, and these accomplishments most often involve change. Sometimes when a minister is called to a congregation, the search committee will give him or her an impressive list of changes they believe are needed. Such changes are usually good and needed in the congregation, but ministers should not assume that all their new parishioners recognize the need for such changes or that they are ready for them. The wise pastor will test the breadth of desire for change among his or her new parishioners before plunging into change that was presented by the search committee as widely desired. In fact, the wise minister will be "taking the temperature" of the congregation throughout the change process and will recognize that it is unrealistic to think we can change everything that needs changing in one or two years. A five- to ten-year plan is usually more realistic than a five- to ten-*month* plan!

Because of the rapid change in our culture, because of the geographic mobility of so many North Americans, and because of the differences among the several generations presently inhabiting the same world, we find more variety of perspectives, experiences, and expectations in our churches than ever before. Such diversity of expectations requires skilled leadership for change.

To pastors, especially, I say, read this book if you believe you are called to help your institution change in significant ways. Otherwise, you may find that the only thing changing is the name of the pastor. The need for change is too great for us to guess at how to lead it. To be as faithful as possible to what God is seeking to do, we need to be prepared as adequately as possible. Chris Hobgood has provided us with a remarkable help in this book. Read it, read it again, and apply it!

RICHARD L. HAMM
General Minister and
President of the Christian Church
(Disciples of Christ)

I would be remiss if I failed to thank the people who made this book possible. I do not have space to list them all, but I ask the eight congregational pastors who are on this list to convey to your partners in leadership my deepest gratitude for open, gracious, and honest conversations. And so:

Gary Straub, First Christian Church, Frankfort, Kentucky.
Laurinda Hafner, Pilgrim Congregational UCC, Cleveland, Ohio.
Randall Spleth, Geist Christian Church, Indianapolis, Indiana.
Tony Stanley, Peoples Congregational UCC, Washington, D.C.
Delores Carpenter, Michigan Park Christian Church, Washington, D.C.
Jack Morris, Largo Community Church, Largo, Maryland.
John Peterson, Alfred Street Baptist Church, Alexandria, Virginia.
Gary Pinder, Lewinsville Presbyterian Church, McLean, Virginia.

Thanks, friends. Please pass this message to those devoted, faithful, and gifted leaders who shared their wisdom with me. Like you, I am glad such people are leaders in the church these days. It gives great hope for the future of Christ's work in this tired world.

CHAPTER 1

Resistance in Congregational Life

And he said, "To what should I compare the kingdom of God? It is like yeast that a woman took and mixed in with three measures of flour until all of it was leavened."

Luke 13:20-21

W hat is this thing called *resistance*? Is it good, bad, in-between or indifferent?

STORIES OF TWO CONGREGATIONS

St. James Covenant Church is a place where, say its members, "yeasty things are happening."

To be honest though, some parts look worn around the edges. The building has stood on that corner for 75 years. This Michigan congregation is a cross-section of generations, including many age 50 and above. Located in a relatively quiet town, the church hasn't seen great numerical growth in recent years.

But that's only the surface view. Beneath those appearances are truly vital life signs. Like a mature person who has no movie star glamour, yet is well cared for with good exercise, diet, rest, and attitude, St. James is healthy and vital. Smiling little children are seated in classrooms or roaming the halls. Youth gather to talk, sing, play, serve, and pray. Adult education choices abound, and the generations do much together. A continuing schedule of activities focuses on providing housing opportunities for citizens of the city and beyond. These range from leading the county's Habitat for Humanity program to sponsoring a team of advocates for public housing to opening space in the church every winter for homeless people.

Worship has undergone rejuvenation in recent years. Once regarded as solely the minister's territory, worship has changed in large part because the pastor of six years, the Rev. Marcia Carrington, undertook to engage laypeople in worship leadership. She had to cajole them at first, but before long they were participating not only by reading scripture, but also by leading prayers of confession, giving the assurance of pardon, leading the Eucharist, and preaching. Now members are eager to take part in shaping and leading the liturgy.

Not widely noted, but clearly critical, is the way leaders have opened the congregation's ways of decision making and problem solving. For years church board members had been chosen from among those willing to plod along and do the same things year after year. Laity burnout and dropout rates were rising. To some the future seemed uncertain, even scary. When Pastor Marcia called for a goal-setting and planning process that would create a fresh mandate for leaders, some active and powerful members objected, fearing big-time changes. A few were willing to allow change in some elements, thinking that they could protect their own most-valued areas. Others said the new initiative was a "slippery slope," that change in one area could in time affect all of church life. Feeling she had nothing to lose and everything to gain, the pastor invited a number of those people and a few newer members to join her in a process of prayerful exploration of the question "Where is God calling us?" Possible opponents became allies as these leaders came to trust Marcia, confident now that she didn't have a prior agenda but simply wanted them to develop their future in the knowledge that their congregation belonged to God, not to any one person or group.

New learning about the congregation's purpose and members' life together has abounded. For example, the people of St. James have found that sometimes a problem is caused not by the issues involved but by the effect of stress in another part of the church, one that seems completely removed from it. They have begun to pay attention to their past—not only to celebrate great times but also to learn about the ways they are likely to repeat mistakes if they *don't* learn from them. They are discovering it is important that leaders have a dispassionate and objective temperament, a willingness to listen as they lead and, if leaders disagree, to do so fairly if they are to be a faithful and productive congregation.

The people of St. James believe they are on a "faith journey" between what is and what can be. Most of all they have fun (they call themselves a "party church"), and they are certain that "yeasty things *are* happening."

High Street United Church is a study in contrast to St. James. Although it is located in a similar kind of city and is about the same age, High Street's vitality seems sapped, as though life had been boiled out of the yeast. No matter how hard the people try, the congregation seems to become more fragile, and the future is filled with questions.

Decisions made by the city had a major effect on the church. High Street had been a major thoroughfare. The adage "location, location, location" as defining the three most important criteria for a new congregation seemed to have received primary attention when this congregation was formed—long before church growth experts had adopted this wisdom from the real estate world. Until a decade ago High Street Church was the "cathedral" congregation in the city for its denomination. But when the interstate highway route cut the street off two blocks west of the church, life changed. Longtime members had to drive two extra miles to get to the church. New people seldom drove by as they familiarized themselves with the city. The church went from high profile to barely visible.

High Street Church's people tried to hold on to their strengths. Before, they'd had creative and inspiring worship and a strong children's and youth program. They were particularly known for their holiday outreach programs, a living nativity and "choir-on-the-lawn." Members were good stewards, believing in the ways their church reached out. The logical path seemed to involve doing more of what they had done so well before.

Ten years later, with numbers reduced by 50 percent and with only a handful of young families remaining, the church was changing. Although they still held to some of the old programs, believing that what had worked yesterday might still work today, their investment and energy seemed to be really tiring. They found it hard to make decisions, often postponing and even avoiding such simple choices as whether to have Sunday school in the summer, or to participate in the community Thanksgiving service.

The remaining members drove much longer distances to get to church, and not just because of the interstate cut-off. In the ensuing decade people had moved to distant parts of the city and county. The church was no longer the hub of members' community. Rather, its constituent community seemed to be shaped like an open umbrella, with the members on the edges and the church in the center. Consequently, members were far less interested in doing ministry in the city. It was no longer *their* city center. One fact illustrated this new demographic reality. In earlier years youth had all known each other through the week as well as at church, because they attended the same schools and lived in the same neighborhoods. Now the few remaining youth went to different schools, had no friends in common, and barely knew each other's first names. Shaping a youth fellowship seemed a daunting task.

This situation faced the Rev. Edmond O'Brien when he came to High Street Church. After six weeks he wrote a letter to his best clergy friend:

> The first Sunday I was here an old man said to me, after worship, "Well, Reverend, are you good at church funerals? Because that's what you're here for." What an encouraging word that was!
>
> I can't say I wasn't warned. The judicatory people told me that the church was on a downhill slide. I read their profile and, as I told you, it didn't look good. But I didn't know how tough it would be.
>
> Pray for me. Pray for us. And give me feedback to let me know if I am getting so sucked into the air of despair here that I become the first line of resistance to any possible changes that will make for healthier life. There will be enough active and passive objection to change—I've already heard the main mantra, "We tried something like that once and it didn't work"—that this church doesn't need me to lead the chorus.

The challenge is great. The leavening yeast appears to have gotten lost somewhere in the kitchen. Yet is not this congregation just as precious to God as any other?

WHEN RESISTANCE COMES

It is easy enough to say that *resistance* is bad for a congregation. It might also be said, however, that if there is *no* resistance in a congregation, then it may be that nothing challenging is going on. Although a statement such as "Resistance is good!" may seem naïve, still I want to pose a central thesis for this work: *Resistance can be a sign of vital, high-quality, and faithful life in a congregation.*

Resistance comes in various sizes and shapes. Sometimes it is focused, as when people flatly oppose changes of important values or policies. For example, if someone wants to develop entrance requirements for new members beyond the particular denominational heritage, then I hope people will resist. If a member or group insists that everyone must exhibit one or two particular spiritual gifts, then those who have a clearer understanding of the biblical meaning of spiritual gifts should resist. Resistance to negative initiatives is a good thing.

My purpose here, though, is not to analyze this form of resistance. It is to explore and understand the kinds of resistance that can arise in response to leaders' strong, mission-focused initiatives. I contend that, quite often, the depth of resistance points to the significance and potential impact of the change initiative at stake. Furthermore, significant congregational change can be helped by well-intentioned resistance and a leadership response that recognizes, learns from, and adapts to positive resistance.

What Is Resistance?

1. *Resistance can be defined as energy that rises up to counteract change in a system.* Congregations, like any other organization made up of human beings, are systems. They are made up of parts that link together, so that the whole is at once the sum of the parts and more than the sum. The whole becomes that sum plus the unique character that is this new entity. In biblical-theological language the whole, or the congregation at its best, can be seen as the sum with the Holy Spirit stirring new life in its midst. It is a wondrous mystery, this whole.

"Systems thinking is basically a way of thinking about life as all of a piece . . . about how the whole is arranged, how its parts interact."[1] It is as though we are part of a fabric of interrelated threads and, as part of that fabric, we don't always see the patterns woven into the whole cloth. We see the part of which we are a part and fail to see the ways these parts are intertwined.

It is in the nature of a system, an entity made up of interrelated entities, to resist change. Systems naturally seek a point of balance, an equilibrium, where the ebbs and flows of living seem to achieve a healthy and active truce. This balance can be seen, for example, in the numerical growth of a congregation. It reaches a certain size, perhaps a comfortable stage at which people can feel nurtured and challenged. After reaching this point, unless a major transformational event takes place, the congregation will likely maintain that same size. To grow much would be disruptive. Obviously, a reduction would also disrupt the congregation's equilibrium.

This is not to say that every system should seek to maintain the same equilibrium at all times. This certainly cannot happen in our minds and bodies: otherwise the baby would not grow up, the adult would not age, and adventures and challenges in life would be nonexistent. In other words, there would be no life, for to live is to experience the push and resistance that come with growth and change.

Hans Selye, a physician who has done monumental work on stress, explains the balance that systems theorists call homeostasis. "One of the most characteristic features of all living beings is their ability to maintain the constancy of their internal milieu. . . . For instance, [one] can be exposed to great cold or heat without varying [one's] own temperature."[2] Selye calls this the "self-regulating power," and whenever it fails, "there is disease or even death."[3]

Social systems act in much the same way. Applied to social entities, homeostasis becomes, according to organizational experts Speed Leas and George Parsons, "the tendency for a system, relationship or organization to mold the behavior of others into predictable patterns, making it possible for us to 'get along,' to do work, to find safety, to trust."[4] Without this inclination, every time we are together we'd have to form relationships all over again.[5] What a task that would be!

But in a social system, when stress from either internal or external sources exceeds the established self-regulating balances, distress occurs. Resistance is a natural response to the elevation of stress. Resistance is not a hostile force, though it can be acted out with hostility. Rather, resistance is a natural response to anything that seeks to disrupt the equilibrium of a system. That equilibrium is experienced by the system and its parts as stabilizing and comfortable, and even at times healthy.

In systems thinking, the entity is most vulnerable to negative "stuff" when it is either stuck in seeming changelessness or is changing the most. In the physical self, a lazy body risks, for example, clogged arteries. At the other extreme, one who runs too far without nourishment risks fatigue at best, shock or even death at worst. In social systems, a community where nothing new ever happens will in time die. For example, the Shakers, already celibate, died out when adoption laws were enacted that made it impossible to depend, as the primary source of new community members, on children orphaned or unwanted and dropped on the Shakers' doorsteps. At the other end, an organization that makes change the name of every game will soon suffer because nothing lasts long enough to give the organization an identity; there is no time of homeostasis for it to settle into being what it is.

Should congregations avoid high stress at all costs to maintain their equilibrium? Should all parts that make up the whole be focused primarily on keeping the organization alive by doing nothing out of the ordinary that would threaten the balance? Should we seek "peace at any price," to borrow a line from the old hawk-dove debates of another era's antiwar movement?

By no means! To focus all our energy on maintaining equilibrium is to fall prey to the notion that change doesn't need to happen. George Parsons points out that "congregations run the risk of becoming stuck in their successes. The newly won ground becomes our home." This "tyranny of successful habits," or overadaptation, can result in staying with a pattern "long past its usefulness," and failing to respond to the environment.[6] Change, however, happens. And if the change is not lived into with a sense of invitation and hope, it may well overwhelm the congregation.

Resistance comes when the stability of the present meets the challenge of transition.

2. *The many places resistance appears.* Any time a disruptive change begins to impinge on an organic system, resistance occurs. Hans Selye speaks of the "stage of resistance" that follows an alarm reaction to agents that can damage the body.[7] A healthy person who picks up a common "bug" begins to develop resistance to that bug. Over time, after encountering several such agents, one begins to develop broad resistance to them and the damage they could cause. Resistance, in this case, is a good thing. Indeed, many years after Selye's work the human immunodeficiency virus (HIV) became known; its major characteristic is to render the human system unable to resist invasive infections that would, under normal circumstances, be treatable by reinforcing the body's resistance. Sometimes only when resistance is lost do we see how valuable it can be.

As in a physical body, resistance in social systems, such as congregations, is significant for ongoing life. We might be tempted to distinguish between resistance to troubling changes and resistance to exciting and hopeful changes, and to suppose that we can "build up our resistance" by addressing only the changes we think of as positive.

Clearly, however, the difference between these two kinds of change is often subjective, deeply tied into our value systems. For example, a church's becoming an open and affirming congregation toward gay and lesbian people can be one person's greatest faith-centered hope and another person's source of deepest anguish about the direction of the congregation. Inclusive worship can, for one, mean incorporating the musical and spoken expressions of all participants, and for another mean simply welcoming all people to participate in *our* form of worship.

I do not want to use this study to sort out which opportunities to develop healthy changes are "good" and which are not. Rather, my purpose is to explore the process of change and the ways in which we can learn to meet resistance not as an enemy but as a sign of life.

Resistance can begin with a variety of circumstances, or forces, outside a system. It can also begin within the system itself. I believe resistance may begin within the very ones who are leading change. If the pastor proposes a vision of a changed congregation, she would do well to explore her own center first, to discern whether she resists the very dream she proposes. This need not be an embarrassing step. The Hebrew scriptures tell the stories of prophets often reluctant to step into the particular breach to which they are called.

Such reluctance may be especially true of the pastor who has been in one pastorate for a long time. In a study of pastors who had been in their settings for 10 years and longer, we found that most got there by offering a caring style of one-to-one pastoral ministry, and were not as eager or skilled to give active corporate leadership to the congregation.[8] They "paid their dues" not by leading revolutions but by being consistent caregivers, day in and day out, who could be depended on for solace, faith guidance, and particularly, supportive friendship. Rocking boats is not easy for these pastors. They themselves resist change. So when change is proposed, one's own resistance needs to recognized and explored first.

Then comes the resistance of those who oppose the initiative of the pastor or other leader. This resistance can come from several sources. One pastor tells me that, as members explore becoming an "Open and Affirming" congregation, most of those who opposed any change were, it really seemed, afraid to give up power or even their place in the congregation's life and structure. Their questions may be simple ones: "Why here?" "Why us?" or, "We ain't broke, so why fix us?"

Others not in formal leadership roles might simply chafe from a feeling of powerlessness. Any move to be different will trigger resistance in them.

Still others will ground their resistance in deeply felt biblical and theological principles. These are often the most difficult people to work with, for nothing gives us greater pause than citing "authority." Sometimes those who believe they know the authoritative sources best are able to resist change readily because they are more secure in their position than others. It helps change initiators as well as resisters to be biblically literate.

3. *Resistance offers an opportunity for learning.* As this chapter is being written, conflict rages between Palestinians and Israelis. They are, quite literally, struggling over a tiny piece of land. Conflict has been described as what happens "when two pieces of matter try to occupy the same space at the same time."[9] For ancient Hebrews, in captivity in Egypt, the land was only as wide as the valley of the Nile River running through a desert. It was understandable that the Hebrews, liberated from slavery in Egypt, celebrated the joy of being taken to "a good land, with flowing streams . . . and honey" (Deut. 8:7-10). This land, deemed broad by ancients, however, seems very narrow these days. *When parties vie for limited space, conflict takes place.*

Quite often in the congregation when change appears, conflict emerges—not as much about literal space as over whose values will be at the center of the community's life. Resistance can be seen as a way of holding to cherished values. What seems to one a disposable part of church life may be precious to another. Such conflicts of values can emerge between generations, ethnic groups, theological persuasions, or political perspectives. They can become focused on how the congregation worships, how much it will grow, how inclusive it aspires to be, or how the physical space will be used.

Once again, we can learn from our mental-emotional-physical selves. When we are under too much stress, when competing forces try to occupy the same space, we will feel the resistance. Whether the stress is brought on by lack of sleep, excessive exercise, bacteria, overeating, emotional overload, weighty decisions, or a myriad of other possibilities, we will normally know, from the messages our bodies and brains send us, when we have reached a maximum level of tolerance.

Can competition of forces for "space" in congregational life bring on stress that tells us that too much is being undertaken? That the system can't absorb all of the changes being proposed? That different directions need to be considered? That other resources are needed to do whatever we are considering? The congregation, like our living selves, has a range of tolerance for change, and to fall below it or to push beyond it can turn normal stress into distress. Extraordinary destabilization can result.

I would propose that some customary ways of dealing with resistance to change—ignoring it, overwhelming it, fighting it, discounting it, demonizing it, to name a few—are not constructive. Indeed, they will lead to even greater polarization in the congregation.

It is important to know that the energy of resistance may have truth to tell us, and that we would be wise to listen and learn. Sometimes, in this listening and learning, we make new friends and allies and find new strategies and ways to change appropriately.

One way of naming the choice that faces us when we encounter resistance to change is to see that the system can be either immobilized or energized by the tension. I want to explore what the latter can mean for the congregation. Let's examine some case studies for insight into resistance and its capacity to energize a congregation.

Studies of Resistance in Congregations
Oak Hill Fellowship Church

The issue for this congregation is "to move or not to move." Oak Hill Church moved to its present site on the city's far edge 42 years ago. At that time the move was a reaction to the changing racial composition of the neighborhood and of the congregation. Leaders believed that new growth would not occur, because any gains in membership would be more than matched by the loss of longtime members going elsewhere. One quiet but courageous African American couple had begun worshiping at the old church. They joined, and were made to feel very welcome. Their joining, however, triggered reactions that led, within two years, to the congregation's moving nearly 10 miles into the new suburbs of the great city.

Oak Hill Church struggled for a few years, then called a wise and effective young pastor. Dr. David Roberts had the gifts to combine good preaching and faithful pastoral care with a knack for leading a congregation whose membership had reached a plateau of about 250, with 150 active participants. Ten years after he came, David led a major building project, resulting in a new and beautiful sanctuary, offices, a good study/meeting room, an efficiency apartment for homeless people, and a reshaping of the old space. This was a challenging project, in large part because of complex negotiations with the county authorities to satisfy codes. The pastor and other leaders were understandably tired and hoped for a period of stability after construction was complete.

With great skill David Roberts enabled Oak Hill to move into a pattern of seeking a future vision and doing strategic planning every three years. Goals and objectives were set, and the congregation grew from success to success. With few programmatic exceptions the church became more and more a place for participants to experience spiritual renewal and opportunities to serve.

Twenty-five years after Roberts's arrival, the church is in an urban, cosmopolitan neighborhood 10 miles in from the city's outer rim. People of many ethnic heritages live in the area, and many find Oak Hill an inviting church. The people of Oak Hill are hospitable. It is beyond their comprehension to turn anyone away. Significant growth has finally begun. The leaders decided to hold two worship services each Sunday as well as taking other steps to accommodate a growing, diverse congregation. Members are committed to ministry and mission where they are.

Two other factors, however, draw the congregation toward a new locale. First, the vast suburbs, growing far beyond the current location, are home to many members as well as to many unchurched people who might be interested in a congregation in their own neighborhood. In addition, the church is "landlocked," limited to a relatively small corner lot with no available space for parking or construction. They have begun to explore a move to a site further out, with five or six acres of land, near the new populations.

As a planning group develops a strategy to engage the people in a decision about moving, they hear these questions:

- Why should we move and take on a huge new debt for land and buildings?
- Who's to guarantee that new people will join us if we relocate?
- What will happen to ministry in this multiethnic community? Do we just leave it to some fundamentalist group?
- Is this move worth the investment of time and money? Can we afford it?
- Is this really what God wants us to do? Does it mean we are running

from, rather than risking, change? Or are we called to stay here and bloom where we are planted?

- We have been doing well in this changing neighborhood, so what's wrong with staying and being hospitable and community-centered as we are now?

Resistance to Oak Hill's proposed move comes from one primary source. Clearly the church is enjoying a healthy, vital, and growing time. There is anxiety that a relocation will result in people turning away and saying, "After all, Oak Hill is moving. Is it really the church for us?" The balance, or homeostasis, that has resulted in a healthy time of life may be lost.

The leadership group can listen to these questions, hear them for their corrective value, and plan accordingly. Or they can respond to these questions like a steamroller, as though the questioners were being obstructionist. What would you do if this were your congregation?

First Covenant Church

The questions for this congregation are "Can we be evangelists? And if so, what does this mean?"

First Covenant began when about 125 people walked out of a church five miles away because they believed the pastor was a power-hungry tyrant. It was a contradiction, they believed, for a minister to seek such control in a congregation that had a democratic polity and a professed commitment to the great Reformation theme of the priesthood of all believers.

These pioneers determined to start their congregation in a booming suburb where any church was sure to grow unless the members literally snarled at visitors! The church grew. Within 10 years it had tripled in membership, a reality abetted by a later migration of 75 additional members from the old church. The future looked bright for this congregation. It now ranked near the top of its middle judicatory's outreach giving lists, had the resources to host a regional convention of its denomination, and had produced from among the parish, in its first 10 years, two young ministers.

First Covenant vaulted through the early stages of growth and became a stable, program-centered congregation. The numbers settled at what seemed a comfortable level. New people joined, but their coming essentially balanced the loss of those who left or died. The pastoral staff now included an associate minister. Regular programs like Christian education were of good quality with well-trained lay leadership. Outreach programs were important, and First Covenant was among the founding congregations of an ecumenical "Community for Christian Action."

Beneath the surface, though, lay troubling dynamics. The pastoral staff had never had it easy. One consultant eventually helped First Covenant to acknowledge that from the outset the founding members had understandably been motivated by anticlericalism. Several people, who were capable middle-level managers at work but had not received hoped-for job promotions, used the church as their venue to compete for power and authority. But a rule of politeness prevailed, so differences were hardly ever aired openly. Still, tensions were obvious. In fact, one younger member, not raised in the congregation, told an outside friend that every time he raised a question in a formal meeting he was stared at and given the cold shoulder for days.

In time the vanguard of founders aged. Some of their children remained at First Covenant, although many left. The age profile tilted more and more to the senior side. A dispute arose over a minister's style and capabilities, and that pastor left. The people of First Covenant were led by an excellent consultant, with whom they had contracted for assistance, to see that they needed a fresh spirituality, skill in interpersonal communication, and a new vision of their future. Because their once-booming neighborhood was now a first-ring suburb and undergoing its third ethnic transition in 20 years, they were faced with new concerns about evangelism. The questions for them were complex and demanding:

- Can we learn to reach people for the right reasons and not just to survive?
- Can't we just ride this out as we have in the past?
- Most of us are getting up in years—aren't we too old to become a new church?
- Why can't we just act as we did years ago? It worked then.

Here we see resistance coming from systemic and, for some, personal fatigue. The dispute over the pastor and the resulting transition, coming after years of holding to rigid patterns of behavior, had led, ironically, to energy—the energy of resistance. These people are tempted to work hard at not changing.

These are just some of the concerns facing the leaders of First Covenant. Now, with a trained interim minister, they have decisions to make and work to do if a new future is to be claimed. Their challenge is to live into a fresh evangelism. Will they? Faced with all these new realities, would you and your congregation? Is this a mountain too high to climb?

Mount Moriah Congregational Christian Church

At Mount Moriah, people ask, "Can an old church learn new tricks? Can we find a new calling?"

Mount Moriah was formed nearly 100 years ago in a gentle town several miles outside the District of Columbia. It was an early "bedroom" community, with public transportation providing access to employment at service institutions and government offices. The public transit went through many stages as years passed—from wagons to trolleys to buses and Metrorail.

Mount Moriah grew with the city. During and after World War I the city expanded, and the church became part of the metropolitan area. With World War II the urban area had sprawled to four or five miles beyond the church. The congregation was strong, midsized (about 300), with its numbers regularly reinforced by influxes of professional people and their families. As government and the state university grew, Mount Moriah grew.

In an act of pioneering commitment, this congregation became the parent of a new church. About 100 members moved five miles further out to begin a new congregation. Seen as visionary and courageous, this step also left Mount Moriah severely weakened. The source of Mount Moriah's recent growth, new people moving to this new suburban neighborhood, were also the founders of the new church, and Mount Moriah lost both numbers and leadership skill.

Mount Moriah went through a time of decline. Many of its remaining members now lived at least 10 miles away. What had been a safe and serene village had become an urban neighborhood. The church, located two blocks from the main road, was hardly visible to most new residents, unaccustomed as they were to the village context that had generated this church. Historically Euro-American, Mount Moriah had long been open to people of all ethnic groups, but being open was not the same as engaging people of color, the church found.

The pastoral leadership underwent changes as well. After a strong pastorate during the time the new congregation was being "spun off," the next pastors seemed more focused on maintaining what was left rather than shaping a new future. Then came Pastor Mac, a man of deep faith and a love for the people that was just as deep.

Pastor Mac had been at Mount Moriah nearly 20 years when two things changed his and the congregation's life. He was attacked one day by a man who broke into the building. For a few days his life was in peril. He chose to stay with Mount Moriah after his recovery. Mac called the leaders into a life of prayer. For several years the elders met weekly after worship for an hour of prayer for the members and the congregation's life. In time a renewed worship life began to emerge. The congregation became an inviting and welcoming place. It was alive.

The core questions on the lips of the longtime members (who were still paying the bills) were such as these:

- Can we change?
- Can we welcome all these different people?
- We're blue collar—are they like us?
- Can we learn new ways of worshiping and serving?
- Why can't we just hold on to what we've had and not become something we are not?

The resistance was a result of fear of the unknown. In their minds those expressing resistance knew that this new openness was right. But in their hearts they were frightened and anxious about the changes this would cause in their congregation. The fear was not just for themselves. It was for their congregation—would it survive these new and different times?

Pastor Mac received most of these questions. He had been the pastor for over 25 years, and members' trust allowed them to express their concerns to him. It was his own spiritual depth that enabled him to hear their anxieties and not take them personally. Some thought the congregation was changing in more ways than were comfortable. But none questioned Mac's faith and love. What would happen next?

The Forms That Resistance Takes

Resistance appears in at least three forms: intentionally antagonistic, emotional and reactive, and rational and probing. These three forms will be discussed in more detail in chapter 2. Antagonistic forms of resistance are best addressed using principles of conflict management. I am primarily concerned with the second and third types. These are not mutually exclusive, and they can be worked with. They come from church people who are loyal and helpfully resistant, and they offer promise that can lead to good decisions about the changes afoot.

I write about these more promising forms of resistance because they're frequently encountered; although they might not debilitate a congregation, resisters can drain our energy and lessen our effectiveness in ministry. As a consequence we often ignore them. The results of ignoring them can be harmful later, as those ignored store their resistant energy for a later (and sometimes more perilous) time.

In Summary: The Danger in Having No Resistance

It is tempting to believe that battles are won when resistance is gone. This assumption can be deceptive. If the pastor and other leaders respond to helpful resistance by trying to beat the resisters down, a lull in resisting activity may follow. But if the beaten people have strong ownership of any part of the congregation's story, their resistance may go underground and await another opportunity to surface, perhaps in a destructive form, as they move from emotional to antagonistic resistance. If managing resistance is always framed by the congregation's leaders as combat, then defeat of the resistance is only a Pyrrhic victory, with a battle won at the cost of the whole war. The resistance goes underground.

The absence of resistance can also signal the absence of concern, challenge, or interest. When no one appears to care, leaders need to know that this attitude can point to problems in the mission of the congregation.

During high-stress times, we imagine that it would be wonderful to live and work without resistance. But if we follow the analogy of a living organism, when there is no resistance, the body is dead; because being alive always creates change, and change always results in resistance.

The pastor does well who, as nondefensively as possible, invites and recognizes healthy resistance. Resistance is both an affirmation of her leadership (that she is doing things worth resisting) and a source of potentially fruitful growth and change for the congregation.

FOR REFLECTION

1   At what times has resistance occurred in your congregation?

2. How is resistance viewed—as hostile or helpful? Irritating or empowering?

3. In what ways has resistance been used to help in your congregation's life?

4. Have you ever resisted the leaders of your congregation? How did leaders respond to your resistance?

5. Discuss the forms of resistance observed in your congregation. When have different types appeared, and how have leaders acted when faced with them?

CHAPTER 2

Face to Face with Resistance

A fable from the Congo, in the heart of Africa, speaks of relationships.

One of the mightiest trees in the forest, the Bokungu Tree was proud of itself and its large trunk. It flaunted its long limbs and beautiful, lacy leaves. One day it looked down and said to the Earth, "Why are you there? Who are you? You can never be as wonderful as I!

"You are nothing. You can't rise up in the air! Why, you are ugly! As for me, just look. I am beautiful. The birds build their nests high in my branches, and sing in my leaves. Monkeys play in my foliage and hide there from the noonday sun. But as for you, Oh Earth, I just throw my worn-out leaves and my old branches down on you that are no longer of any use to me."

The Bokungu Tree tossed its fine head. Some old leaves fluttered off and a dead limb fell to the ground. It made the tree look more beautiful, for now all its leaves were fresh and its limbs were sturdy.

This went on for a time until the Earth became provoked. One morning the Earth said to the Bokungu Tree, "You claim to be so beautiful, but where do you get all your life from, except me? If it were not for me holding you up and protecting your roots, besides giving you food, where would you be?"

But the great tree would not listen. It kept bragging about its great strength and beauty and laughing at the Earth. So the Earth decided to teach the proud tree a lesson. She called her Soldiers, the Driver Ants, and also the Termites. The Earth said to them,

"Now go to work and dig the earth away from the proud Bokungu Tree, and eat the dry roots."

So the ants made a large nest under the tree, which removed the dirt from the roots, and the termites then ate the dry and lifeless roots.

Then the leaves of the great tree began to fall off and the branches fell one by one. Finally just the bare trunk was standing. Then came a strong wind and the once proud Bokungu Tree fell to the Earth.[1]

Like all fables, this one doesn't speak to all of life, but it contains strong truth. One of its truths is that the interests we hold in common are often more important than those on which we differ, and that wisdom lies in looking for those we share.

WHAT IS RESISTANCE RESISTING?

Most resistance in congregations happens because people have common interests but different approaches to addressing them. The exception is strong antagonistic resistance, and I will come back to this type shortly.

Resistance doesn't happen on a whim. It is a natural part of life. Organizations react to change just as physical bodies do. That they react at all is an important sign of life in a collective body like a congregation.

Resistance is a natural response to change in biological and social organisms (organizations). Almost at the time of an organization's birth a tension is born between what appears to be the need to carry out the mission that brought the organization into being and the pressure to stay alive and stable. The former requires continuing change as the organization adapts to new demands, resources, challenges, and visions. The latter depends on maintenance of the status quo, and holding all the parts in stable relationships.

Figure 1

(a) The need for stability versus (b) the ever-changing mission

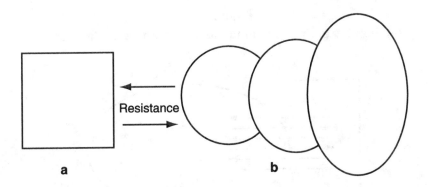

Resistance

a   b

The boundaries of the stability-seeking side of a social system (a) seem fixed, predictable and unmoving. Those of the mission-focused side (b) appear flexible, ever in a process of growing, changing to whatever the organism is to become.

Although tension between the need for stability and the need for change exists in any living system, we refer to that tension as resistance when accommodation between the two has to be intentionally sought. Accommodation can cover a range—from resolution and new solutions, to compromise, to an agreement to disagree. Sometimes there is no accommodation. It is my hope to increase the possibility of accommodation somewhere along this range.

As one who spent years in the "b" camp above, disdaining all factors that spoke of maintenance and stability, I have often been swamped by the uncertainty that comes when these powerful forces lead to a kind of organizational tug-of-war. In retrospect, that sense of being overwhelmed came because I, among others, believed that stability is "bad" and change is "good." Is there still time to confess that I was, at best, naïve, if not flat wrong?

The truth in congregational life is that both of these dimensions are essential; the resistance that comes when they tug on each other is natural and vital. We would do well to seek ways for the congregations of which we are a part to learn to cherish the vitality that can come when creative tension is managed with prayer, care, and skill. Thanks be to God, the great

Bokungu Tree and the Earth can learn to live well with each other. Most of the time, they do just that!

Figure 2
(a) Stability and(b) changing mission in a healthy tension

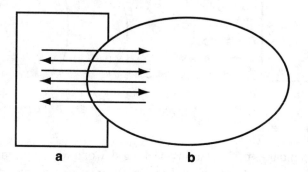

a   b

THE SHAPES OF RESISTANCE

Resistance doesn't come in only one form. At the same time, it is not a commodity like potatoes or oranges that can be sorted into sizes, shapes, and qualities. It exists in degrees and shades. We will examine some of these. The most important fact about resistance is its source, or the systemic situation that gives it birth and energy. Knowing the source helps us see the level of investment that resistance claims in people. First, though, it is important to recognize that some resistance is really antagonistic activity; otherwise we may spend time and energy responding to antagonism just as we would to other resistance. These responses will not be effective with antagonism. This, then, is a word to the wise.

1. Antagonistic Resistance

"This pastor is simply unacceptable. He is foul mouthed, narcissistic, won't listen to others, and can't preach. I will not rest until he is gone. I've gotten rid of ministers before, and I can do it again." The last part is the antagonist's threat.

Such antagonism can be devastating, its aim being to win at all costs, with nothing short of destruction as its method. I made a phone call, and it verified the woman's claim that she had indeed organized the opposition to a minister in another congregation in another state. Shortly thereafter, he was fired. There was little doubt that, if not confronted, the woman would do it again. She had already begun challenging other members to support her effort. Several people, participants in her prayer group, had, after she had won their friendships, signed a petition for the pastor's dismissal. The phone call affirmed a virtually identical "m.o.," or modus operandi, in that earlier congregation.

Antagonism of this depth and force is a particularly virulent form of resistance. It cannot be countered by the means that will be discussed in this study, as I intend to focus on kinds of resistance that can be learned from, lived with, and at times engaged in decisions about the congregation's future.

Antagonism at the level illustrated is a sickness. It takes no genius to know that most pastors and lay leaders do not have the training necessary to face down such an effort to win and "take no prisoners." Space permits me to say here only that congregations that meet such antagonism should normally seek outside assistance as soon as possible.

2. Sources of Resistance

In a physical body resistance comes when the system is pushed to change beyond its range of tolerance. That is, the system's normal functioning will be disrupted. A woman works long hours, and her mental capacity, diminished because her brain lacks oxygen, gives way to fatigue. A man runs 10 miles one day when he is accustomed to running only five miles daily; with the depletion of certain chemicals, his legs begin to cramp.

Similarly, organizations meet resistance when the system is pressed to act in ways it has not acted before—to change beyond its capacity for change—that is, in a way that significantly threatens the system's need for stability.

When Central Church decided to lease its parking lot to a developer who wanted to construct an apartment building, resistance erupted.

"Where will *we* park?"

"What if we need to expand our facilities?"

"This is the only land we own. We're giving it up for 99 years!"

"This new pastor won't listen to us experienced members."

The anxiety created by the envisioned loss of stability, the breaking up of the "even keel" on which Central had been riding, generated strong resistance.

At Happy Valley Church the congregation had undergone a rapid change. Most new members of the past two years were young African Americans. The longtime members, almost all of them Euro-Americans, rejoiced in the energy and vision brought by the new people. Yet as they began to look at a transition necessitated by their pastor's call to another ministry, one veteran member was heard to mutter to another, "We may be losing control around here." This signal of coming resistance appears to have its source in the ambivalence felt about changes already happening. These changes seem to be welcomed on one hand but feared on the other.

University Community Church had gone through its best stewardship and outreach year in a decade. Visitors and new members were coming in good numbers. The youth and young adult groups were growing and doing exciting new programs that challenged members to be givers and not just receivers of God's grace. In the midst of this activity Pastor Mark and the executive board called for a new mission identification and planning process in the conviction that the future is best charted from a position of stability. After all, when it's possible, preventive medicine is far better than waiting to become ill and having to seek a cure! However, predictable resistance arose because some were convinced that to talk about tomorrow when all is well today was asking for disruption of the creative stability. Again, what we might call "disruption anxiety" generated resistance.

After a period of prayer and reflection, the elders and pastors of St. Michael's parish challenged the congregation's members to undertake a new emphasis on evangelism. Workshops, church socials, bring-a-friend Sundays, special Bible studies, and a seeker-focused service were planned. But the planning team, chosen only from the elders and pastors, had persistent difficulty recruiting others to help carry out these events. Finally, after low participation over two months of these activities, the emphasis was called off. Bitterness was expressed by leaders, but most of the people just shrugged it off. Resistance had taken the form of apathy that went back to the reality that all the new projects were planned with no voices outside the leadership team called on for their opinions. Only when it came time to act were others asked to work. Here the source was clearly lack of investment by members at large, because they had not been trusted to have any judgment or part in the very idea and its planning. Resistance took the form of "intentional apathy" (perhaps an oxymoron, but maybe not).

Sources of resistance can usually be identified and even anticipated. If this information is belittled or ignored, resistance is likely to expand to fill any space available in the system's life.

3. Some Characteristics of Resistance

I use the term "characteristics" guardedly, having already declared that resistance cannot easily be sorted into sizes and shapes. These measurements are, therefore, quite subjective, rather like the famous expression of a Supreme Court justice that pornography cannot be defined but that one knows it when one sees it.

It is helpful to assess resistance in two ways: the *kind* of energy it generates and the *interests* it seeks to assert. To do this, continua are useful:

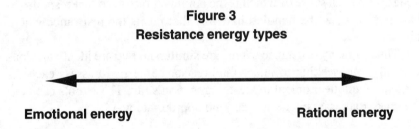

Figure 3
Resistance energy types

Emotional energy   **Rational energy**

Both emotional and rational energy extend the full length of the line. What varies is the degree to which a particular resistance is driven by energy of one or the other. The continuum tells us that rarely is only one type of energy generated. No point on the line is better or worse than any other. That isn't the issue. What matters is that both the leaders or others who initiated an action and those resisting seek to sense the kind of energy that is happening. Quite clearly the appropriate responses vary, depending on whether the energy fueling the resistance is strongly emotional or highly rational. This is the value of the emotional/rational continuum as a way of assessing resistance. Responding to emotion-driven resistance with rational arguments will probably be futile and might make the situation worse. Likewise, it is rarely helpful to respond to reason-driven resistance with emotional appeals. When we understand the source of resistance, however, we can respond in a way that will enhance the system's health.

Figure 4
Resistance interest types

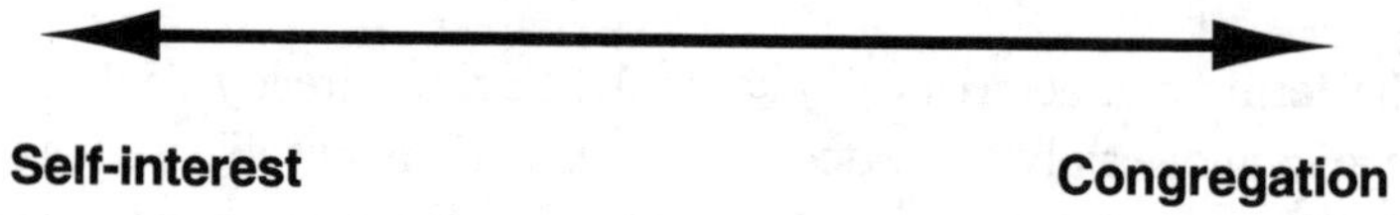

Self-interest   **Congregation**

Again, resistance is not rooted entirely in either self-interest or congregational interest. It leans in one direction or the other, and is unlikely to be located right in the middle. This statement is not meant to cast judgment on either type. Self-interest and congregational interest can both be valid concerns in matter of stability versus change. It can be immensely helpful, though, to have a sense of which is the dominant factor, so that response to that resistance can be handled in a way that meets the resistance where it is.

Though many resistance events are similar, no two are identical. Consequently, one seeking to understand resistance needs to assess each instance as a unique moment in the congregation's life. These tools can help you make that assessment in a fair and appropriate way.

A MODEL FOR UNDERSTANDING LEADERSHIP AND RESISTANCE

Resistance in the congregation happens in response to events. These may be sermons, particular leadership roles or actions, individual programs or policies, or initiatives (I use the term "interventions" here as well) that leaders or others undertake to bring about change in the congregation. To see the place of resistance, I want to offer a model, tested informally with 50 pastors. They see in it a helpful way to view initiatives and resistance in a congregation's life. It shows varying degrees of initiatives (interventions) that can be taken by pastors and other congregational leaders As movement goes deeper into interventions, resistance will grow in intensity.

Figure 5
Degrees of change and levels of resistance

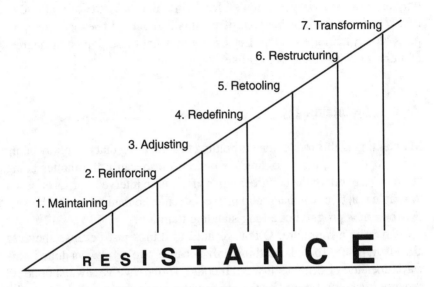

I experience resistance that can fit various descriptive characteristics just discussed happening at all seven points of initiative/intervention. It is not the kind but the *intensity* of resistance that changes as the degree of intervention increases.

POINTS OF LEADERSHIP INITIATIVES/INTERVENTIONS

We now take a journey through the seven points of leadership initiatives. We will see with each the possibility of overuse. Each degree can also meet resistance of equal or greater intensity. A discussion and delineation of the intensity of resistance will follow the seven points.

First, a definition: *A leadership "initiative" (also called an "intervention") is any action proposed or taken by congregational leaders that may result in change in the congregation's life.* Such initiatives differ in impact, or depth, and thus in the degree of change that may result. Let me say that *this is not a linear succession of interventions.* That is, one type of intervention is not in itself better than another. The test is the appropriateness of the intervention for the particular situation. Keep this observation in mind, for we'll come back to it after looking at the intervention points. Know also that even when an intervention is focused on only one part of a congregation's life, it will affect all parts of that body's life. Whenever anything happens, it eventually touches life everywhere. All parts of a system are related. Let's see now what these points, or degrees of initiatives/interventions, look like.

Point 1. Maintaining

Maintaining in this model means holding to something that is already being done. At its best, this "holding" is undertaken because the matter being "held to" is good for the congregation's life. It is an intervention, as opposed to simple inaction, when a group actively decides to maintain something. It may be a new program or a long-standing tradition.

There is a trap here. Often we hold to things just because they are already in place. To do something only because "we've always done it this way" does the effort little justice. It could be that "we've always done it" because it's a good thing for the quality of the congregation's life. On the other hand, if the only reason to do something is because "we've always done it this way," then we should consider not doing it any longer. *Maintaining* can certainly be overused.

If something that we are already doing holds meaning and promise for the congregation's life, then a decision to keep doing it can be wise. In this scenario, establishing it as a repeated practice certainly seems appropriate.

First community Church planned a party for Mrs. Hinsey's 90th birthday. The celebration was particularly joyous because it came in the middle of a very cold and depressing January. The annual birthday party became a tradition, in time becoming (see *reinforcing*) a celebration of all birthdays (Mrs. Hinsey's, of course, was featured until her death at 102).

Will there be resistance to *maintaining* interventions? If there is, then this resistance is more likely to come form those who want greater change. When resistance to maintenance appears, it will generally be more passive in nature, aimed not so much at stopping something than at just not actively helping to maintain. "Passive" resistance means not acting to help an intervention come to fruition, while "active" resistance would focus on intentional activity against an intervention. We will see, as the points of change deepen, that the greater resistance will be active and will come from those who want less change.

Point 2. Reinforcing

Reinforcing, a step beyond maintaining, results from a decision to strengthen a particular process in the congregation's life. This reinforcing activity may concern an ongoing or a new issue. While it may seem like splitting hairs, the important difference between maintaining and reinforcing is that in the former the decision is simply to keep on doing that one thing, while in the latter additional resources are committed to an effort.

The reinforcing action may be a call for more people to carry the program, for added finances, or for increased prayer and attendance.

A reinforcing initiative can come when a particular program is seen as benefiting the church, or when feedback suggests it *will* provide benefits. Wilson Memorial Church helped one youth with limited finances to attend a summer conference. She returned with such enthusiasm and willingness to work in the church that "scholarships for summer conferences" became a line item in the budget. Potomac Avenue Church allowed space for the housing of homeless people during a bitter cold spell one winter. So many people stepped up to help that housing homeless people in winter became a regular program.

Reinforcing will sometimes meet resistance both from those who want more change and those who might be skeptical of change. A reinforcing initiative normally doesn't ask for the kind of long-term institutional commitments that will raise major resistance. On the other hand, reinforcing decisions often follow events that are not part of a long-term plan (who planned for the particularly cold winter that created the emergency for homeless people?), and can raise almost instant resistance. Here resistance may become more active opposition to an intervention, depending on the issue (housing the homeless resulted in more active opposition than did putting camp scholarships in the budget), though much of it will remain passive.

It's important here to say that reinforcing bad practices can become one of the church's deadliest habits. It often happens because a decision is not made to do anything to change the bad practice. When resistance to reinforcing initiatives comes, it is wise to ask this question: Is the resistance telling us that we are reinforcing a bad habit? More often that not, this kind of negative reinforcement is less an intentional decision to act than simply a choice not to do something. But the very action of doing nothing can give added strength to a negative practice.

Old Brother Jack was the greeter before worship for years. As he aged, he became more careless and would say and do things that troubled many. After a jolly "hello," he often criticized the choir and pastor to visitors. He was overeager to hug women, including first-time visitors. No one wanted to confront Jack. People valued his willingness to greet. Good greeters were hard to find. It wasn't long, though, before the hospitality team, on seeking feedback from visitors who didn't return, found that Brother Jack was a detriment to a good practice. It took some courage, but he was finally asked to move over, either in his methods or his presence. Grumbling all the way, he chose to yield the door. The congregation needed to reinforce hospitality at the door, but had to stop reinforcing negative ways of welcoming worshipers.

Point 3. Adjusting

An *adjusting* initiative is one that doesn't change the overall direction of a core emphasis, but that calls for altering one or more aspects of an emphasis already present.

One congregation has long held to the practice of offering varied worship opportunities. For three decades, either by intentional decision of the governing body or because no one decided otherwise, a "contemporary" worship service has been offered, usually adapting to whatever style of music and communication is current. In the '60s and '70s, it was folk music. In the '80s light-rock Christian music was used. The '90s saw praise songs and nonreligious terminology being employed as a "seeker-sensitive" worship service was developed. This congregation has a long history of adjusting. Indeed, a norm of adjusting prevailed, sometimes intentionally. This norm's importance has been reaffirmed at times. From time to time the congregation has been asked to remake the decision to offer worship choices. It always has affirmed the practice, without hesitation, though each time a fresh decision was made over the years the same core group of worship "traditionalists," as they proudly called themselves, questioned the need for this alternative worship opportunity.

Adjusting is a regular practice in healthy congregations. Without it a congregation won't be able to adapt to new circumstances. Whether the change affects a highly visible area like the worship example cited, or less threatening areas, like maintaining the food pantry or the frequency of congregational fellowship dinners, many congregations make adjusting one of the basic elements of their planning. At the same time, it's important to know that adjusting can be overused, to the point that it becomes more like tinkering. The difference between real adjusting and tinkering is seen in whether any qualitative effort is made to refine or upgrade the particular practice. Tinkering, like most "busywork," is soon seen for what it is—time and effort spent with no improvement seen.

Again, the key to an *adjusting* initiative is that it does not change the core emphasis—it simply makes alterations in the frequency, times, or focus of that emphasis. Adjusting is still a fairly low-grade level of change. An adjusting change process might, for example, seek a new focus for adult education, a fresh network for homeless ministry, or a different approach to using the media for communication within the congregation's membership.

Adjusting will produce some resistance, but as long as it seems to embody "safe" changes, the resistance will not be major. In a long-term adjusting process like the contemporary worship example, some of the same people and issues will rise up, as in that congregation, to resist each new adjusting initiative undertaken. Most resistance here will be questioning of cost, feasibility, and other pragmatic concerns. "Can we do this in a reasonable way and at a low cost?" will be one of the key queries to adjusting initiatives.

Point 4. Redefining

We begin now to move into degrees of change that can alter the congregation's landscape. *Redefining* calls the congregation's people to examine basic assumptions about why we do what we do. It is a higher-risk venture, because it can bring a change in focus resulting from a changed sense of mission.

Downtown Community Church found its worshiping congregation becoming far more racially and culturally mixed as the surrounding community changed. Where it had been a center-city church for suburban middle-class worshipers (with a membership map shaped like an umbrella), now it was an urban congregation for a cross-section of the city's population. The question now facing this church was whether to call as its pastor a person of color and, with that call, to begin conducting the regular worship in new and multicultural ways. Rather than simply offering a contemporary option at a different hour, the church was now grappling with a deeper change issue.

Orange Community Church was a congregation deeply engaged in ministry and outreach to the hungry and disenfranchised in its county-seat town. Members had tried to be faithful to this call for many years. In fact, older members could not remember when they'd had a different style. The pastor, sensing that the aging congregation was tiring and losing energy, urged parishioners to undertake a process that could result in changing their direction. Early in the experience the people began to see the possible implications for change. They gathered demographic information from the community, finding a significant unchurched population, with many children and youth having no place to go after school. This activity helped them understand the increase in juvenile crime in Orange.

As they grappled with scripture and data, and prayed individually and together about God's call to them, a redefinition of their community outreach began to emerge. They determined to be a congregation in which people of all ages, both within and outside the congregation, could find a place to learn and grow in their knowledge of the Bible and its applications in life. This decision led to many changes in scheduling, hospitality, and particularly, leadership needs. They were faithful to the new call. Even those who said they were "old dogs" were willing to learn "new tricks" as they undertook fresh training programs so they could carry out their newly defined mission.

Redefining moves beyond adjusting: whereas adjusting may alter an aspect within a focal area, redefining changes the focus area. Thus a group within, or even the whole congregation, may sense that it is called to a new way of engaging in its mission. Resistance to redefining will most likely come from those who have a particular investment in an existing focus. The resistance may be assessed using the two continua discussed earlier, emotional/rational and self-interest/congregational-interest. Keep in mind that resistance might come from folk who simply need to defend what has happened, because any change makes them feel as though they are questioning the faithfulness of the church through the years.

While redefining change is major, it does not reach the point of structural change. Any felt threat from redefining change will be in those who have been particularly involved in prior emphases and who hold to them either because of emotional ties or out of a sense that the emphasis is still needed. As a result, a congregation may order its life to continue doing at least some of the prior work. Such decisions call for wise assessment of resources so that both focuses, the former and the new, receive the attention needed to be done well.

It is wise to beware, though, of over-redefining. Some congregations have gotten into a cycle of redefining their focus every time someone grumbles about something, or every two to three years simply because "it's time." At such times it may be more appropriate to reinforce or adjust than to redefine.

Point 5. Retooling

Retooling goes a step beyond redefining. It takes new goals, hopes, and dreams, and crafts existing structures into forms that can support these fresh ways.

In the world of industry, it is important to note that "retooling" need not mean making a plate from a pot, or a plowshare from a sword. I describe retooling as making an old tool into a new one that does the old tool's task in a new way. Retooling does not invent new devices to do new jobs. Rather the new tool is used to do the old job better. If in the retooling a new horizon opens up, then God be praised. Typewriters gave way to computers. The Pony Express had a brief life, with the telegraph's invention rapidly making it a relic. Speed won the race, for wires were even faster than ponies.

Retooling addresses distinct areas of a congregation's life more than it does the whole life of the church. As in a machine shop, retooling takes existing parts, crafting them into tools usable for a new future. It does not make over the whole engine, but the brakes might well be re-engineered in a way that makes them work like new brakes.

For many years King Hill Church chose both deacons and deaconesses, each with distinctive missions. The deacons served the sacrament and collected the offering. They were often called on to do maintenance work on the church's physical plant. Occasionally they'd be challenged to give leadership to the stewardship campaign, and once they were formed into teams with other lay leaders to help clusters of the congregation's members become centers of caring, service, and fellowship. The deaconesses prepared the sacramental elements and cleaned the equipment, organized hospitality for bereaved people, and took turns preparing coffee and juices for a fellowship time after worship.

Challenged to reflect from a biblical perspective on their roles, the two decided to become "the diaconate," with about as many members, but now able to distribute the jobs and even more tasks across a gender- and age-inclusive group. They learned that women *can* serve communion, and men *can* prepare coffee. By retooling across gender lines they used their human resources in more faithful and productive ways.

It is at the point of *retooling* that the old saw "If it ain't broke, don't fix it" most often comes into use. Neither the deacons nor the deaconesses were "broken." For all most folk knew, they were doing their job. Why upset a floating boat? Resistance here will be active, often because those who resist have a viewpoint limited in large part by their circumstances.

But it is also important to know that retooling needs to be more than experimentation. Experimentation is important at times, and may be essential to testing the effectiveness and acceptability of change and therefore knowing what really can and needs to be retooled. It is important, though, that retooling be perceived not only as a process whereby we come to understand what we need to do, but also one of doing it. If it is less than that, then it could be seen as a gimmick and will damage existing parts of the congregation's life, certainly including some that are working well.

Point 6. Restructuring

One way to describe *restructuring* is that it is about as far as we can go without turning the whole system upside down. In contrast to retooling, which focuses on one area of a congregation's life, like the diaconate, restructuring dares to look at wholesale remodeling of the way we are organized to do our mission and ministry.

Restructuring must therefore first take seriously the church's mission. Restructuring that has integrity will grow out of a deep sense of what our mission is to be. If we are to hold to the ancient adage that "form follows function," then restructuring is what we do with the form after we have explored our function.

To do honest restructuring, we must first grapple with the question "What is God calling us to be and do as a congregation?" Anything less than this question will be seen by people with any gumption at all as just tinkering. This is not a time for people who just want to mess around with organizational relationships.

Restructuring may or may not be needed when a congregation hears a call to its new mission. If the current structure will provide the essential framework for implementing that mission, then a congregation should stay with it. In a sense, this is as much a restructuring decision as one to change the way we are shaped.

For many years some denominations suggested particular structural forms for congregations. These have often served congregations well. But in recent years, as many congregations have been more deliberate in seeking to discern God's unique call to them, they have found that those prescribed structures were inadequate for doing the unique mission to which they were called. Too often congregations have found themselves bending their program to fit and serve a structure, rather than creating a structure that supports a purpose. This is where meaningful restructuring needs to happen.

Broad Avenue Church was a team player, a denominational supporter that worked hard to follow the larger church's recommended organizational procedures. At a time of particular public social change Pastor Charles asked the congregation to enter a period of serious study about the renewal of the congregation. For nearly two years a group of 30 laypeople explored biblical, theological, sociological, and spiritual resources to seek direction about the congregation's mission. It was an experience that led many people to be willingly committed to genuine exploration of their congregation's mission. In time they made restructuring decisions to carry out their new mission. If they'd not been called to this point, exploration alone would have sufficed, but it would not have culminated in restructuring.

Point 7. Transforming

Beyond all the other levels of intervention, *transforming* turns the congregation upside down. This level of initiative is taken to call a congregation to a whole new self-awareness and commitment to its mission. Often the result of transformation is that, for the first time in a long time, a congregation has a sense of "mission." Transformation is rebirth. Transforming can come from unpredicted sources, or as a result of the congregation's explicit decisions.

Just three months after the new young pastor's installation, Third Street Church's building burned to the ground. This once strong congregation had been struggling to survive, and one of the hopes for the new pastor's ministry was that it would result in fresh energy and growth. Three months into his pastorate was too early to make lasting judgments about long-term effects, though many of the people were feeling fresh excitement. Some older members were suspicious of the young man, though, and weren't ready to jump into the new wave. Then the building burned. Amid occasional attempts at humor ("You set this fire, didn't you, preacher? Just to light us up, right?"), the people looked at the ruins and wondered, "What next?"

Pastor Jefferson, they soon discovered, was a blessing to them. Responding to his leadership, Third Street Church was soon shaping a new identity based on growth and community ministry unparalleled in its denomination. Within five years, outgrowing its new building, the congregation bought a school across the city and moved. Now with thousands of members and a ministry involving hundreds of members and staff, they were becoming a transformed church. At times in this process there were holdouts, people who simply couldn't adapt to the sudden changes. It can take many ocean miles to turn a great ship around. Likewise, the processes that lead congregations to major decisions can take time.

In another place, New Spirit Church was trapped in a dying shell. Its building, programs, and membership were declining. That a congregation so near death bore the name "New Spirit" was an irony lost on no one. The parish called a part-time pastor, agreeing with another small congregation to share the leader. Particularly frustrating was the process of negotiating Sunday worship times so that Pastor Wilson could preach at both churches and have a little time either before or after worship to meet and greet people and hear their concerns.

After two years Wilson decided to approach the parishioners of New Spirit with a proposal that they "go for broke," taking all their savings and investing them in a three-year do-or-die attempt to revitalize. After much prayer and dialogue, the decision was made to take this faith-risk. Believing it to be God's call to them, members asked Wilson to be their full-time pastor. They suspended their constitution's structural forms and set up a small "management team" to work with the pastor to make urgent decisions when needed, rather than to postpone them until a larger governing group had a scheduled meeting. With these changes they have undertaken to read and study as much information as can be found about the re-formation of congregations in decline. This step has not been taken without resistance. In fact, one member of the management team has been particularly vocal in questioning the value of the process. Tensions in the management team have run high at times. The fact that has moved the group through these times has been the shared belief that maintaining the former status quo would have meant the death of the congregation. Time will yet tell if this transformational attempt will work.

Here are two examples of *transforming*. One bore fruit; the jury is still out on the other. Both, though, make the point that this level of initiative calls for the virtual remaking of a congregation. As we will see in a later chapter, congregations far more viable than either of these are undergoing such life-changing transformative processes. A congregation need not be in utter decline for such change to happen. The critical element in transforming change is that the congregation discover a sense of mission and reform its life to carry out that mission. I understand transforming to be that process and time when a congregation begins to feel itself drawn to a particular mission, and decides to commit itself entirely to living that mission. Whether from crisis or intentional decision when times seemed well, transforming means a willingness to die in order to live again. It cannot happen unless it is taken as a profound step of faith.

Once again, resistance will most likely come from some who feel they helped bring the congregation to its present place or from parts of the congregation not ready to pay the price of transformation. The source of the first type of resistance might be the resisters' high investment in things as they were or their fear of change. The source of the second kind can be disruption anxiety. A truism about the degrees of intervention is that some people seem to have a sixth sense about the degree of change facing them, and their resistance rises to a comparable level. Transforming initiatives will always draw resistance of the highest intensity.

LEADERSHIP INITIATIVES

As stated, an initiative is *any action proposed or taken by congregational leaders that may result in changes in the way the congregation lives.* A deeper look at the systemic nature of leadership initiatives is now needed as we examine, in particular, their capacity to elicit resistance in congregations.

Any Initiative Can Lead to Another

We could easily assume that leadership initiatives as described above happen only in a stair-step fashion, making, for example, *restructuring* more "advanced" than *adjusting*. This is not the case.

These seven leadership initiatives are related. In the next chapter we will see that members of congregations interweave the initiatives. Quite often they spoke of one initiative leading to another. These relationships are not always sequential. If, for example, a *restructuring* initiative results in important decisions and changes being made, then often this restructuring will be *maintained* or even *reinforced*. If a congregation risks *transforming* steps, it follows that aspects of life may need *adjusting* or *retooling*. Any initiative can create a loop back to an earlier level to secure the new steps taken. Furthermore, a step taken at one level may hasten movement to a deeper level.

Faith Church undertook a major structural review, in the context of a process of prayerful discernment of God's desire for the parish. It resulted in a powerful *transforming* season in its life, in which the character of the congregation changed in its demographic makeup and in its programmatic and liturgical life. Seen through a systems lens, all these levels are interactive. As viewed in the design, the web is complex. In reality it is far more so, because the loops are endless.

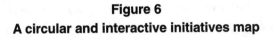

Figure 6
A circular and interactive initiatives map

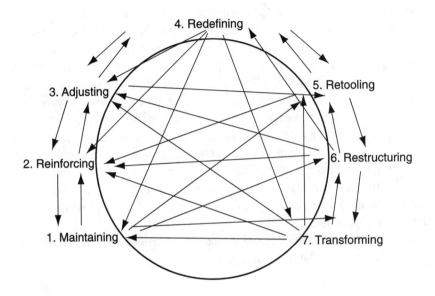

Resistance Increases as Initiatives Deepen

Resistance intensifies as the initiatives move toward greater change. Although we should not expect to find a one-to-one correspondence between specific levels of initiative and resistance, I have chosen to identify seven levels of resistance, each a typical response to the leadership initiative of the same numerical degree.

Most resistance generated by maintaining and reinforcing tends to be passive. *Passive* resistance here, not to be confused with the nonviolent passive resistance of the great protest movements of the 20th century, is resistance that gains strength from inactivity. When you don't like something, don't support it. Intentional passive resistance is sometimes called apathy. I believe this is a misnomer. When people don't act to support something, it doesn't necessarily mean they don't care (this is apathy). It may mean they think their best way to respond is to choose not to respond.

As the potential for change grows, resistance can grow to *disengagement.* An individual may choose to disengage, apart from choices other people make, or he or she might invite others to join the disengagement. Either way, disengagement is an intentional action, and the resister normally makes the action known. Disengagement is pulling back, not yet from the congregation, but from a particular activity or program. "I have some different ideas about the adult education program, but since we seem to be going different directions, I'll just stay out of it for a while." That statement describes resistance by withdrawal. My experience tells me that selective disengagement is used more often than most other forms of resistance. It gives a person a way to declare concerns without giving up his or her voice and stake in the whole system. It may well be a form of *loyal opposition*, a potentially helpful response when the possibility for change deepens. For loyal opposition to be helpful, it must be heard. Then those who question or have other ideas will enter the conversation, now engaged because they see that genuine change may come about if they participate. *Waiting it out* and, finally, *threatened departure* are resistance methods that signal that one is moving beyond loyal opposition to choose a course other than what this congregation intends to do.

The levels of resistance and typical responses at each level are outlined in the chart on the following page.

Figure 7
Levels of resistance in congregational life

Resistance	Initiative	Passive/ Active	Range of behavioral responses in resistance	Hoped-for benefits
L1	Maintaining	Passive	Apathy	Valuing an important program
L2	Reinforcing	Passive/ active	Apathy; questioning	Cooperating to strengthen good parts of a congregation's life
L3	Adjusting	Passive & active	Passive disengagement to limited cooperation	Partnership to identify and address needed adjustments
L4	Redefining	Passive & Active	Withdrawing, friendly questioning	Congregation cooperating in craft identity
L5	Retoolng	Passive & active	Loyal opposition, willingness to compromise	Sharing, discerning new forms of action together
L6	Restructuring	Active doubled	Loyal opposition, active disengagement/ "wait it out"	Deep mutual understanding & work to find new directions
L7	Transforming	ACTIVE	Loyal oposition, threatened or real departure	Working, risking, daring to disagree, trust grows

Ideally, leaders seize the moment of resistance to redirect the ideas and energies of resistance for the congregation's benefit. Changes will happen, and the resistance that results from these changes can be used to deepen the congregation's commitment to its mission.

LEADERSHIP AND RESISTANCE

A continuing, influential factor in this *initiative >< resistance* process is the leadership of the congregation, clergy and lay. Leaders are the initiators, the ones who make interventions that will either change or hold the congregation in place. Leaders are the ones who respond to resistance to change. Leaders are also quite often those who resist those initiatives. So far I have spoken about leadership without defining it.

"Leadership is the art of creating a working climate that inspires others to achieve extraordinary goals and levels of performance" (Gen. John Michael Loh, U.S. Air Force)[2] It is the craft of "creat[ing] an atmosphere in which people can give their best. This allows great visions to become reality."[3]

Atop these descriptions I would add that *good leadership in a faith setting is doing what needs to be done to bring other people to a common goal, consistent with the basic values of love for God, others, and oneself.*

A leader in the Judeo-Christian tradition is willing to step out ahead of others and to be followed, yet does not act as though he or she is "ahead" of others. The leader respects those who follow, is their servant first, trying to meet their needs, yet always yearns and seeks to enable the community to reach a vision of a better place. A leader tries never to ask others to do what he or she is unwilling to do.

Leadership and Management

Often leadership and management are confused in the minds of people in organizations. Such confusion is certainly common in the church, where day-to-day operations require skills different from those that enable and empower people to move toward a new vision and future. Warren Bennis, in a classic text, *On Becoming a Leader*, contrasts the two essential roles.

The manager administers; the leader innovates.

The manager is a copy; the leader is an original.

The manager relies on control; the leader inspires trust.

The manager imitates; the leader initiates.

The manager does things right; the leader does the right thing.[4]

Leadership Styles

Various researchers have identified four basic styles of leadership, which bear a wide assortment of labels. I call them *telling*, *selling*, *facilitating*, and *collaborating*.[5] Proponents of an approach called "contextual leadership" propose that each of these is an appropriate style of leadership when and where it is needed.

Telling is a way of leading that involves just what it suggests: that the leader dares to tell others what he or she sees and thinks. In the church there are leadership functions, such as preaching and some teaching, that involve "telling." Some traditions vest canonical (legal) authority in clergy that requires a "telling" style. Sensitive preachers do not take their "telling" responsibility lightly. When they "tell," the act should come of deep personal struggle, experience, and conviction. "Telling" in this sense is not bossing people around—it is witnessing.

Selling calls the leader to use persuasive methods to win others to be followers. Unlike telling, selling often lays out options, shares experiences, encourages dialogue, invites sharing of values and opinions, and then asks people to decide.

Facilitating seeks to give power and skills to others, with the goal of sharing public leadership with others. The leader is not just a passive observer of the group's life, but also an active catalyst who seeks to empower members of the group to use their gifts, which might include leadership. The leader tries to help others learn and use leadership skills appropriate to the situation.

Collaborating is a mode in which the leader becomes part of the group, using his or her skills to make it possible for leadership to emerge when and where it is needed. The leader is most focused on not being the recognized leader. He or she works invisibly to make others visible. This is not an egocentric move. It is the art of giving others the power to step forward. Why? Either because the ones helped to step forward can, from this encouragement, develop and practice new skills, or because the group's aim will best be achieved with others leading.

Contextual Leadership

In my denomination's ministerial "search and call" process, a minister offers a broad self-description to be submitted when being considered for ministerial positions. Both the candidate and the individuals listed as references are asked to appraise the person's leadership skills by ranking those skills as follows:

_____ Takes primary leadership responsibility
_____ Gives responsibility to lay leaders
_____ Shares responsibility with lay leaders

It has long been the contention of many of us that, because these are not particularly deep and broad descriptions of leadership, a fourth line needs to be added:

_____ Uses whichever style fits the situation

Flexibility is paramount. The good leader learns the range of skills and styles and is able to use whichever is most fitting. This is not manipulation—it is good leadership. The best leaders are people who have more than one method available. Contextual leadership uses whichever skills are most needed to lead in the situation at hand. Congregational leaders, both those who initiate changes and those who resist, serve more faithfully and effectively if they are able to use a variety of skills at appropriate times and places.

Initiating the Initiatives

A leadership initiative or intervention is any event, encouraged or started by a congregation's leaders that has the potential to bring about change in the congregation. One of the responsibilities entrusted to leaders is to see the whole life of the congregation as well as the parts and to care for the relationship between the whole congregation and its parts. Leaders, in other words, give care to the health of the system. Does it need to stay in a stable place for a while? Does this part, that part, or the whole need to change? If so, how much change is needed, and can be absorbed? Asked in a framework of prayerful reflection, these are church leaders' key questions.

Leaders can't control everything about congregational change, nor should they try. The church belongs to God. Leaders have trusteeship for a while. What leaders can do, with prayer and hope, is initiate changes that will help the system and its various parts achieve a healthier state. Some powerful realities need to be kept in mind as leaders do their work.

Congregations change. A proposition: the congregation without initiatives is mired in mediocrity, racking up reasons to be called irrelevant, and heading into decline. Yet the impulse of all systems, congregations included, is to maintain stasis, or balanced stability. In spite of the latter, we find that biological systems change—a fact as natural to them as the stability impulse. Similarly, social systems, like congregations, change just as much as they need to maintain stability. Neither biological nor social systems will stand still, however powerful that impulse may be.

Leaders, aware of this tendency, have the task of giving definition to the congregation's changes. The alternative is to allow change to happen *to* us, but without helping it happen. Healthy congregations experience unplanned and planned change. The leaders' task is to make the planned changes as faithful to God and helpful to God's church as possible, and to respond to the unplanned changes with similar faithfulness.

The timing of initiatives is important. Though timing is not everything here, it is certainly to be heeded. It might not be wise, for example, to propose a bold initiative in capital development at the same time the congregation is undertaking a discernment process on an issue such as being an Open and Affirming congregation related to gay, lesbian, bisexual, and transgendered people. Timing is also as much about how many initiatives can sensibly take place at any one time. Looking to the congregation's history for insight about its range of tolerance for change is one place to begin determining the best timing.

It is important to know what level of initiative one proposes to enact. Identifying the seven types of initiatives described in this chapter enables leaders to make wise decisions about the type of change needed and the tolerance of the congregation for change. In systems thinking, stress that can push the system inordinately above its tolerance level is understood to be unhealthy. The range of tolerance, or "what we can take," is generally wider than we assume. When one first begins an exercise program, he or she is warned (often in labels on the equipment at the fitness center) to see a doctor before making a major increase in physical activity. Congregations also need to "see a doctor," so to speak. A congregation that has been fairly placid for some years, doing only *maintaining* initiatives, may not be ready for an initiative with *transforming* potential until it has first grappled with *adjusting* or *redefining* some dimensions of its life. Wise leaders look at the vital signs of the congregation (stewardship, participation, consistency of involvement, willingness to risk) as they try to determine the tolerance range. Sometimes it is best just to ask the people. Leaders then plan to push a step or two, at most, beyond that range.

How Does a Leader Respond to Resistance?

The *initiatives><resistance* picture is incomplete unless we discuss the leader's response to resistance.

   Anticipate resistance. I have discussed several kinds of resistance, as well as passive and active resistance. A wise leader will anticipate the kind and intensity of resistance to an initiative, and then plan to respond to resistance that is a notch higher. Thus, if an initiative falls into the *adjusting* field, the best strategic move is to be prepared to respond to those who believe that their congregation's life is being *redefined*. Why? According to what I call the "slippery-slope theory" of active resistance, most people when considering a change will ask, "Well, if this change is made, then what will be next?" Meet them on that slope and be ready to respond to their concerns, activities, and energies. The best response may simply be to calm fears by assuring them that nothing will be done until everyone has an opportunity to share in the decision. Then ask them to name "what next" and invite them to take part in shaping it.

Face-to-Face with Resistance: A Summary

In this chapter we have explored resistance, or the way a system responds to efforts to change the balanced equilibrium that is a natural and healthy part of all biological and social systems. But because all systems must either grow and change or die, that stasis will always be upset. The challenge for congregations is to plan for change through knowing the points and depths of initiatives, or interventions, that leaders can make.

We need also to be aware of the responsibility of a leader to take initiatives, knowing that there are important factors to consider:

- The congregation without initiatives is a congregation in decline
- The timing of initiatives is important
- Knowing the types of initiatives is essential
- Anticipating resistance is wise

It is particularly important to anticipate a degree of resistance described by the "slippery slope theory."

Resistance can be met with an open ear, with the sure knowledge that if a leadership initiative meets resistance, then the initiative may have some substance and value.

FOR REFLECTION

1. Identify some times in your congregation's life when maintaining, reinforcing, or redefining initiatives have been undertaken. What happened?

2 How might you have prepared yourself and your congregation to face resistance?

3. An exercise:
   - Ask people to form pairs and face one another
   - The partners should face the palms of their hands towards one another's palms without touching palms
   - One person begins to move his or her hands in varying patterns
   - The second person reacts to the first partner's movements and initiates other movements
   - Ask group members to talk about how they respond to these "hand movement initiatives" and to leadership initiatives

4. Define resistance.

5. Define congregational leadership.

CHAPTER 3

Clergy and Lay Leaders at Work

Congregations and other institutions formed by people of faith seem seldom to move into the future in long leaps. It is more likely that movement happens in stops, starts, spurts, and sudden lurches. When it happens, it is with faith that God is already in the future calling us ahead. One place to see this steady movement at work is in the lives and ministries of clergy and lay leaders of growing congregations.

Congregational growth, as I use the term, has several dimensions. In my 20 years of ministry in one congregation we found that the areas of compassion, spirituality, stewardship, and evangelism were the focus of the congregation's energy. These areas are remarkably parallel to Jesus' personal growth, described in Luke 2:52: "And Jesus grew in wisdom and in years [in stature], and in divine and human favor." This framework of growth was later used for self-assessments of 70 congregations, and found to be a helpful way to reflect on the sometimes baffling theme of "church growth." The congregations whose case studies follow are all growing in at least three of these four dimensions. They have learned that the growth that takes its strength from God's power has, like a cut diamond, many facets. Like the interior of a house, it looks different when viewed through different windows. But when these dimensions are brought together, we have a diamond, a house, or a congregation that has many useful and appealing qualities, which, we hope, are at the same time unified. Thus one way of seeing the unique nature of each congregation is to examine the specific ways in which that congregation grows and the skills used by leaders in response to resistance. The goal is for pastors and lay leaders to learn and practice skills needed to lead change and respond to resistance in healthy, fair, and hopeful ways.

CONTENT AND METHOD OF CASE STUDIES

In this chapter I will tell about eight clergy and their lay partners who have given focused and devoted leadership in the growing congregations they serve. The pastors are among 32 clergy whom I interviewed for the book *The Once and Future Pastor* (Alban Institute, 1998). The eight case studies are of clergy still serving the same congregations.

For each case study I conducted several interviews with lay leaders as well as with the pastor. When possible, I observed meetings and other events in the congregations and did considerable reading about the congregation and particularly this pastor's tenure. While this is not an empirical study, as the sample was not large enough to produce data that could speak for a larger whole, still it tells, in anecdotal fashion, the stories of clergy and laity who have learned to lead. I believe that one of the best ways for us to learn is to follow those who have successfully blazed trails that appear to take us to our destination.

One of the rich results of this experience for me has been to see that, even in these times that are deeply unsettled for many congregations, there are clergy and laity leading the church into the next part of its history, and they are enjoying it.

PRAYER AND DIALOGUE
First Christian Church, Frankfort, Kentucky
The Rev. Gary Straub, pastor

First Christian Church was born in the mid-19th century, one of the most important efforts of organizer and first pastor Phillip Fall. Fall was an important frontier faith leader of the Christian Church (Disciples of Christ).

Frankfort is Kentucky's capital city, located between Lexington and Louisville, the state's major economic and cultural city centers. Frankfort has always been respected but not adored by the whole state. Kentucky's near neighbors—Tennessee, Indiana, Ohio, and West Virginia—all have capitals in strong cities: Nashville, Indianapolis, Columbus, and Charleston. Not so with Kentucky.

In a similar way, First Christian Church has had an important presence but has not been the most visible of Disciples of Christ congregations in the state. It is medium-sized and has strong, respected clergy and lay leadership. It is a solid programmatic congregation. First Christian has quietly stood as a stalwart voice for faith in a small city preoccupied with public governance. Three clergy served long and faithful pastorates from the 1940s through almost the end of the 20th century. First Christian Church was the kind of congregation that gladdens the hearts of denominational leaders by practicing good stewardship, fostering enough evangelistic growth to maintain its size, and providing modest numbers of lay and clergy leaders to serve the larger church. Also, no major disruptions occurred. In the mid-20th century, what more could be asked of a congregation?

The Rev. Gary Straub came in the early 1990s. He found a church that was aging, both in membership demographics and attitude. For decades First Christian had held high that good reputation of being dependable, unspectacular, and faithful. This congregation had cared for its own—but Gary found its own becoming weary of caring.

Gary had been the pastor of congregations in Chattanooga and Memphis, Tennessee, before coming to Frankfort. There he had enabled elders (an important lay leadership office for Disciples) to develop programs for growth in spirituality and leadership skills. At the same time he had encouraged people to do mission through the congregation's life—not only using traditional organizational steps such as those recommended by denominational resources, but also calling out and training the laity for ministry based on their spiritual gifts.

Gary's call to Frankfort meant changes. He brought questions: Where are the youth? Why do young adults seem less willing to commit themselves than older ones? Are we enabling people to identify and use the gifts God has given them? In a world that no longer thinks the church is special, can the church still be special enough to appeal to unchurched and younger people?

Gary is a soft-spoken, easygoing man with a ready smile. He conveys serenity and an assurance that he really cares about the individual. He is a person of deep spiritual discipline and conviction. He and his wife have built a retreat hermitage on their small farm north of Frankfort. They welcome guests to relax, rest, and pray, alone or with others.

Rather than an entrepreneurial congregation-builder, Gary sees himself as a deep foundation-planter. He believes that he cannot do ministry alone. Early on, he asked the Frankfort congregation to call Bill Bingham, who had been his associate minister in Memphis, as a co-pastor. Gary and Bill are truly partners, each bringing special strengths and a vital role in a partner-leader process that has as its core goal enabling laity to do ministry.

This kind of pastoral leadership was new for First Christian. From a traditional dependence on the clergy for those matters called "ministry," First Christian Church was being led to be a community where all members are engaged in ministry. For example, the SHAPE program (Spiritual gifts, Heart, Abilities, Personality, Experiences) is a three-part process. People are invited to discern their spiritual gifts, meet in a small group with others who have done the same (to deepen understanding of the shape of their gifts), and finally to meet with a "ministry outfitter" to discover places in which to serve. The program has helped people lead in stronger ways within the congregation's life. One retired couple served in the denomination's overseas ministries. The identification of spiritual gifts is changing lives.

Other initiatives have been taken by Gary and his fellow leaders. Perhaps the most far-reaching is the emphasis placed on prayer. Since Gary's early years as pastor, prayer groups have been at the vital center of the congregation's life. For four years the elders have met weekly for an hour of prayer and teaching. Gary invited them to "pray for what's on the back of your eyelids," a metaphor for one's issue of greatest concern. As well, programs like one called "Training of the Twelve" are used. This program invites 12 new (or potential) lay leaders to identify their gifts and be part of a group that explores themes like biblical study methods, denominational history and beliefs, leadership skills, and spirituality. Such leader development methods, says Gary, "have moved the congregation from low expectations—too often we expect mediocrity—so that we now expect more."

Gary called "unapologetically," as he put it, for members to begin tithing. This emphasis has resulted in significant growth in stewardship, enabling the construction of a new building with space for nurture and community ministry.

The central focus for the leaders of First Christian Church is on developing all members as ministers. Using a team-based approach to shaping the congregation's life in what is called the New Horizons project, leaders invite the people to allow their gifts for ministry to "bubble up." They keep a "bubble up" chart where members record their spiritual gifts and their uses of gifts. Said Gary: "Sometimes we've had the right people in the wrong places." The value of this chart has been limited so far, as people are still becoming accustomed to taking spiritual gifts seriously, but the leaders hope that it will be a useful instrument for an even more useful leadership emphasis.

Lay members speak with great appreciation of the congregation's deepening spiritual life and other changes:

- "We were a congregation at war with itself. This has changed."
- "Heart-to-heart talks about our differences got stuff out."
- "We're willing to let go of bad ideas and programs. This is different."
- "If Gary had not come, we would still be where we were 20 years ago."

The consensus of lay members placed the changes in the range of levels 3 to 5 on the chart. One said, though, "We are on the front edge of level 7 transformation."

This growth has not been without cost and resistance. Lay leaders offered several observations about the nature of the resistance:

- "Resistance is here. Taking a traditional, well-established congregation requires rising up to reach to those outside the established leadership. There will be difficulties due to change."
- "My own resistance made New Horizons difficult. I wasn't sure about the openness of the group, whether my input was really wanted."
- "The New Horizons team assumed that people's giftedness would produce team leadership. What we failed to do was train. We need to get people to actually step up and act out their spiritual gifts."
- "People in state government don't easily work in teams. [This] mentality creates resistance. . . . In [an old congregation] no one is ready for change. Older members ask why."

The resistance to change ranged from personal reluctance to a belief that the congregation's whole life would be negatively affected. Some would not buy into supposedly new ideas (for example, spiritual gifts, partnership in leadership), while others simply renounced any efforts at change in the tried-and-true traditions.

It is also important to listen to the laity as they speak of Gary's leadership style and his integrity and demeanor in response to resistance. All lay leaders who talked with me said that from everything they had seen and heard, Gary is the same person and leader with his closest friends as with a group from the congregation. His ways don't change when resistance becomes overt. Listen to them:

- "He has taught us to disagree lovingly. This has been our most significant change."

- "He has taught us about vision-casting."
- "He is a seed-planter; he has an authenticity that sustains us all."
- "His spirituality [reinforces] everything he does."
- "He brings routine things to prayer."
- "He teaches us by example that when we stop praying, the momentum to do what God calls us to do ends."

Gary meets resistance with an invitation to prayer and dialogue. He refuses to compromise his core beliefs in the laity's gifts to be ministers. He has focused on the elders and the emerging New Horizons teams to be the new leaders in a congregation that has long been governed by "functional" committees and other relics of a time when the whole capital city of Frankfort knew about First Christian Church.

An Analysis of Resistance and Response

Resistance in First Christian Church has been active, though not focused on particular programs as much as on the dynamics of change in the congregation. No one event seemed to galvanize massive resistance, but as several processes tended to increase the pace of change, resistance has grown. The source of resistance here is the way change is perceived by some to destabilize the long-term balance of the congregation.

Gary's way of working with resistance has been to anticipate and prepare for it more than to react. Teaching and "vision-casting" are important in the leaders' ministry, though the primary tool in the face of resistance has been to bring the differing voices together through prayer and dialogue. A step at a time, Gary and lay leaders have led in what is, at minimum, a long period of restructure. If indeed, as one lay leader stated, "We are on the front edge of transformation," then the resistance level can be expected to rise, for resistance increases as the degree of change deepens. Gary and other leaders of First Christian Church will probably find that the best preparation cannot prevent high resistance but can help them deal with it. What we do not know is whether the approach of "let's pray and talk together," which has served quite well in response to resistance to changes in the 3-to-5 range will be enough when transforming work is being done.

The growing skill of Gary Straub and his co-leaders (Bill Bingham and laity alike) to anticipate points of resistance can be a useful tool. Because increasing resistance can be anticipated, a similarly growing climate of inclusive dialogue can be an important method, not to disarm possible resistance but to hear the voices of resistance as the congregation's future is being shaped.

PASTORAL CARE AND COURAGE

Pilgrim Congregational United Church of Christ, Cleveland, Ohio
The Rev. Laurinda Hafner, pastor

When the Rev. Laurinda (Laurie) Hafner preached her trial sermon at Pilgrim Congregational, 32 people were in worship. Twenty-six of them made up most of the remnant of members still at Pilgrim, and the other six were "friends who had come to talk me out of accepting the call," Laurie recalls with a chuckle.

Once the largest Congregational church in Cleveland, Pilgrim had, like many other urban congregations, deteriorated. Though it had been strong and influential in the past, change (its own and the community's), had left it fragile and virtually powerless. For nearly 10 years Pilgrim Congregational Church was listed by the United Church of Christ as "an available pastorate," and it had a search committee and an interim ministry for that entire time. It was far from being the great pulpit and pastoral center it had been in the first half of the 20th century. A collective depression seemed to hold this small community in its grip.

Members say that persistence may well be Laurie's middle name. "She works so hard that we respect her," said one laywoman. It was clear that Laurie also "works smart." That is, her ministry is always focused, intelligent, and aimed at achieving growth in commitment, numbers, and strength. Attendance now averages nearly 200, and membership stands at 400. This congregation, which once had over 1,000 members, had dropped to almost none. The 10-year renewal has been impressive.

When Laurie was called as pastor, the sanctuary pipe organ had been unused for 20 years. She encouraged an early decision to seek funds to repair and begin using it again. That done, the organ became, as she had hoped it would, a symbol for the revitalization of much of the rest of Pilgrim's life. "It was an early, bold goal," said John, a musician in the congregation.

For Pilgrim, though, revitalization didn't mean just restoring things that had been done in the past. Members, long-term and newer, speak of Laurie's vision of a congregation reaching out in creative and caring ways to minister to the needs of the city's people. The Tremont area is an old Victorian part of Cleveland, separated in later years from the rest of downtown by interstate highways. Once a center, then a fringe, Pilgrim's neighborhood now has a new future as the arts are emerging in businesses, in restaurants, and at Pilgrim Congregational Church.

Several benchmark decisions and the resistance that resulted are notable. Seven years ago, at Laurie's initiative, the congregation undertook a yearlong study of biblical understandings of human sexuality. Various interpretations were welcomed and discussed. Some minds were changed. Becki and Nancy, who joined shortly after Laurie became pastor, described her way of engaging people in that study and other processes. "Surprise doesn't work well here," said one of the pair. "Laurie spends much time thinking about things before she verbalizes. She communicates with key lay people and develops lay leaders."

Near the end of the study year Laurie preached a message on what it would mean for the congregation to be Open and Affirming—that is, accepting of gay, lesbian, bisexual, and transgendered people. (In the United Church of Christ, this term denotes a formal process and organization. In some other denominations, the term is used generically.) Laurie's sermon dealt with the gospel's call for the church to include all people. Saying clearly that she understood those whose interpretation of the biblical point of view differed, nevertheless she called the congregation to support a decision to become part of the Open and Affirming movement. They did.

"I am justice oriented; it is a defining quality for me," Laurie said. The congregation's debate over the issue of whether to become Open and Affirming was the primary justice issue in her early ministry at Pilgrim. It has been significant in Pilgrim's growth, as a number of newer people have joined—not only those who came because of their sexual orientation, but also others who were drawn by their respect for a congregation willing to make such a public declaration.

Certainly there was resistance to this change. Several people left and others, particularly some long-time members, opposed even the study process. The year of study, entered into without preconceptions of the stances people were expected to reach, was vital, and it engaged some who had objected. Said Ron: "People are willing to change a lot more when they like—and trust—you. Laurie is a master at managing change. She is there with you." An honest blend of personal affection, genuine charm, and a

courageous call to new directions is ascribed to Laurie by several laypeople. "I pay my dues with pastoral care—not to manipulate, but because it is right," she said. Such care makes an important difference when a congregation faces change.

Other decisions that sparked resistance, yet resulted in changes, include opening the building to the arts. Three theater groups are now housed at Pilgrim, using space there for rehearsals and performances. The church also is the site of concerts, featuring children's programs performed by the famed Cleveland Orchestra.

Thinking about the culture of defeat that she found initially, Laurie speaks with delight about Pilgrim Congregational's hospitality. The church has a "Good News" team that happily and proudly welcomes and follows through with visitors. Just about anyone who comes to worship has been invited by someone who is already a member. What a change from the Pilgrim Congregational Church of a decade ago!

Laurie's description of her leadership and pastoral style is congruent with those of lay leaders who spoke with me. "Smart pastors don't play favorites. I like people and try to build relationships. I am willing to be bold in witnessing."

"With Laurie we get big doses, a saturation, of pastoral care," said Marilyn. "She's always there for an individual," said Becki. Margaret, an octogenarian and senior member of Pilgrim, said, "Laurie recognizes people who accomplish things, and she gets people interested by inviting them to work in the church's process." John described the greatest change at Pilgrim: "The study process [on human sexuality] redefined the congregation; it transformed this church."

When asked specifically about the way Laurie has worked when faced with resistance, one representative member of Pilgrim said, "Laurie just bravely moves on. She doesn't let it daunt her. Laurie always tries to find laypeople who are excited about a project so they can share her support of it."

"She is unafraid to address resistance," Ron said. "She turned what could have been a real negative into a bonding experience by her advance work in the Open and Affirming process and decision. She builds relationships with a winning personality, and she sets the energy level."

Laurie knows how to call the congregation she serves to be prepared to engage change and thus to face resistance. She said of both herself and Pilgrim, "When I started, we had nothing to lose by doing what we set

out to do." She understates her own courage, because it is clear that had all of this not worked, her career would have been damaged, and perhaps the legacy of Pilgrim ended.

What is it like at Pilgrim now? This is an unassuming, egalitarian church committed to serving Christ through loving God's people and creation. The Rev. John Thomas, general minister and president of Laurie's denomination, is a member of this congregation. Laurie says that his regular duties "include unplugging commodes and, in particular, taking care of my little girl during congregational activities."

"We have parties all the time," Laurie said. "We party just about every time we meet." One is led to believe that those are not just rowdy parties. There is much to celebrate at Pilgrim Congregational United Church of Christ.

Analysis of Resistance and Response

Laurie's ministry has been all the more remarkable because the congregation was deep in crisis, nearing death, when she was called. What I believe can be seen in her ministry is the importance of the craft of preparing the congregation through pastoral care and teaching for a transforming level of change, and the courage and grace to meet resistance when it comes.

Combining the boldness to speak the word and to do it with love, Laurie, perhaps unwittingly at times, appears to disarm resistance before it mobilizes. She is a good listener who is willing to hear good ideas that come with resistance, but she does not compromise her convictions in the process. She seems quite skilled at meeting high-level resistance by reaching to include even the most vocal in communication about the future. While often disagreeing with the premise articulated, she often wins the resister. In the Open and Affirming process several of those who resisted became engaged when they realized that for Laurie "inclusiveness" meant including current resisters in the congregation as well as new people who had been previously excluded because of their sexuality.

Early resistance at Pilgrim was passive but willing to wait. This attitude is described as in the 1-to-3 range (see fig. 7, page 41). Stronger resistance began to mobilize during the human sexuality process. The year of study and the openness of Laurie and lay leaders engaged many who were resisting; when their concerns were heard, protest became somewhat muted.

Since then, the resistance appears to have been of a kind that seeks to offer good ideas to the process, whatever issue is at stake—a healthy sort of resistance.

LISTENING AND BUILDING TRUST
Peoples Congregational United Church of Christ, Washington, D.C.
The Rev. A. Knighton "Tony" Stanley, pastor

If any congregation in the nation's capital has, for much of the past century, represented the strongest aspirations and hopes of the African American community, even in the face of open and uncompromising discrimination, it has been Peoples Congregational United Church of Christ. Its history is the story of a powerful and sometimes stormy marriage of a great city and, some say, a greater congregation. For decades the church has given leadership to the city through outreach ministries and advocacy for causes that were not always popular. From Peoples have come many leaders to hold appointive and elective offices in the District of Columbia.

It is not typical for a congregation as large as Peoples Congregational (2,000 members, with 900 in worship each week) to feel like a family. But it demonstrates the openness, frankness, and genuine mutual affection that characterize strong families. When there is disagreement, it is not experienced as a crisis; rather it is like "a family argument," as one leader put it. In the work of this congregation we see that just as a small ("family-sized") church can have as much dignity and impact as a larger one, so a larger one can foster close personal relationships. The fact is, Peoples Church is a large congregation, and its governance and witness reflect a more complex congregation, even as intimacy among members persists.

Formed in 1891 as an African American breakaway from a Methodist Episcopal Church, Peoples' history takes the faith path of many African American congregations in cities like Washington, D.C. Initially they were an oppressed people seeking their own religious expression. They became a congregation with the courage and wisdom to do risk-taking outreach while not attracting attention in a climate that didn't welcome visibility by black congregations. Thus they came to be an active, freedom-focused community of faith. Peoples Church has lived a powerful history of oppression, aspiration, liberation, and always restlessness with the status quo. As a rule the church has been led by pastors with long tenures, and community ministry has been a dominant value.

The Rev. A. Knighton "Tony" Stanley came as Peoples' pastor in 1968. He had gone to Yale Divinity School and then became a campus minister who advised students protesting racial injustice. A time as associate minister in a large Detroit congregation helped him understand urban ministry. He felt ready to assume this important urban senior pastorate. Pastor Stanley, known to his members as "Tony," described his relationship with the members of Peoples this way: "I listened; they trusted."

The congregation has undergone major transitions during Tony's pastorate. He describes the broad framework of his ministry as "rather conservative—worship and praying, teaching and learning, caring and serving, growing in [the] Holy Spirit and spiritual depth, and becoming a tithing congregation." A more precise description than "conservative" might be "fundamental." That is to say, for example, if throwing, running, receiving, blocking, and tackling are fundamental skills for playing football, then the words Tony used describe the "fundamentals" of a faithful congregation. Early in Tony's tenure Peoples Congregational Church began an ongoing planning process that has been important for congregational life. The transitions described here are outgrowths of that process.

Not long after Tony's arrival the first major transition of his ministry began. Peoples Congregational was born of a passion to be free. Members left their parent church for this reason. A congregation of African Americans who lived in a city of deep, punishing racism, Peoples was a bulwark of early black pride. It was made up of middle-class black people who had done their best in the face of personal prejudice and institutional racism. Refusing to be victims and choosing to be people of faith, they bore their burdens bravely, and thus Peoples entered a changing world in the 1960s and 1970s. Before, they had lived under oppressive laws. The laws were changing, and the members of Peoples were ready for this new context.

Tony came shortly after passage of the civil rights bills of the mid-1960s, the first major movement away from Jim Crow segregation. Washington, D.C., had been doubly affected by generally accepted cultural racism *and* the absence of self-government (a policy widely viewed by black people to be part of the same old pattern of racism, but described by people with power as merely a political matter).

The first major transition in the congregation was in directing evangelism to a constituency whose employment level was moving higher on the economic scale. Tony notes that when he came, Peoples Church had many government employees in its membership, the highest-ranking having reached only level G-9, or middle-level civil servant (an employment classification of the Federal Civil Service). After he came, and because of newly won civil rights laws, civil service levels of African Americans entering government service—and joining the congregation—rose. Young adults were among those advancing and being invited to join the congregation. "Older ones, just as brilliant, were resentful," because they were stuck in lower-level classifications, said Tony. They had done their very best and had made amazing gains *for their time*. Their resentment about the younger, newer members often crystallized into resistance. Tony held regular conversations with the leading voices in the older and younger groups, seeking to engage them in dialogue on mutual goals for Peoples Church. It was during this time, when "all of them had a sense of having my ear," that mutual trust, which has characterized Tony Stanley's ministry, was born.

Another major transition concerned property and buildings. Peoples Church moved to its present location in 1954, purchasing an existing building. In Tony's first year, 1968, ground was broken for the Arthur Fletcher Elmes Center. Named for the beloved pastor who had served Peoples for 37 years (1926-1963), this facility houses conference, education, fellowship, and office space. In the late 1970s growth and sensitivity to the need for worship space accessible to those with disabilities led to a plan to build a new sanctuary. A decision was made to model this space after an African hut design, raising fair resistance. Considerable education and interpretation won many to the concept. Nevertheless, there were losses, but the sanctuary, a strikingly bold structure, was completed and continues to serve Peoples Church well.

In addition to these evangelistic and building initiatives, important outgrowths of the ongoing planning have been new developments in Peoples Church's outreach and worship ministries. Still a force in community life, with prominent District of Columbia leaders in its membership, Peoples Church continues to have an outreach program that touches many. Worship opportunities range from traditional to jazz and healing services. There has been wide acceptance of these initiatives, and they are seen as ways of doing outreach.

When asked about the levels of initiatives described in chapter 2 (see fig. 7, page 41), Tony and lay leaders expressed differences of opinion about changes in Peoples Church's transitions. As a rule (with the exception of the change toward a younger membership), lay leaders tended to regard the initiatives as deeper than did their pastor. Both pastor and lay leaders avowed that the early time of change was at levels 6 and 7, largely a transforming experience for their church. Tony described the building (particularly the sanctuary) experience as ranging from level 3 (adjusting) to 6 (restructuring), while lay leaders affirmed it as at least a restructuring time (6). Tony rates the ongoing planning process as level 4 (redefining) to 5 (retooling). The lay responders speak of it as a continuing transforming (level 7) experience.

From another perspective, Tony believes that everything he does holds the potential of engaging each of the seven degrees of initiative. He described, for example, the preparation and execution of the building program as covering the range from 3 to 6, but some aspects of the effort reflected lower or higher levels of resistance. From him we can learn that many lasting initiatives do cover a range of degrees, and we cannot always know how far they will move on the scale. But the pastor said that if he finds himself promoting level 1 initiatives, *maintaining*, to the exclusion of the others, especially in his ministry, then "I hope I'll have the good judgment to get out of here."

Tony's self-description as a pastor and leader reflects a refreshing blend of self-confidence and modesty. He speaks of his "conscious use of evenhanded pastoral care," and says that he "errs on the side of confidentiality, never telling others' business or engaging in gossip." He works consciously at developing leaders, with his primary method being "coaching and on-the-job training." It is important to Tony "not to need anything from people, yet to need them all, and to develop a reverence for who they are."

Lay leaders affirm most of these qualities, but again it appears that, by comparison, Tony understates their views. Said Althea: "Tony has a demanding way about him. He doesn't listen to gossip or innuendo. He's a dreamer and an artist who can see the whole thing in his mind's eye; he sees them different from most of us."

Bradley pointed particularly to Tony's knowledge of the congregation and his being a strong pastor who "seems to know everybody." Constance spoke of him as a "model person for people to look up to, and he is very spiritual; he says God stays with him at all times." Said Ivy: "He takes you to his heart. He is my minister and friend. He has earned my love. He always has us in a training, praying, teaching mode, in which he is leading, guiding, pushing, pulling, but most of all nurturing us." Tony tends to a less flattering self-description, saying, instead, "I have just been doing my job, what is expected."

Analysis of Resistance and Response

In assessing Tony's approach to resistance, and the approach that he trains lay leaders to take, the pastor and lay leaders agree. One lay leader said that Tony has "an open door to all, no matter [members'] opinion of something he has upheld." This evenhanded fairness gives believability to the openness. Tony said that he finds ways to "pay for changes," by going as a pastor to all groups in the church, not just when change is under way, but in steady times as well. Lay leaders speak of the importance of the ongoing planning process for encountering resistance, because it gives all voices an acceptable means for addressing decisions about the future.

In particular the generational changes that came in Tony's early years as pastor provoked resistance. Tony continued to honor the opinions of those troubled by this change. But when the changes began, they knew he had a sense of vision about where the church was called to go. Similarly, some older folk resisted the building of a new sanctuary, not only because of the architectural concept but also because of the price tag. Taking on such a financial burden was a new thing for a congregation with people of limited means. His pastoral care for them again won the day, helping them know that they weren't being left behind, that their caution and judgment "were appreciated," as one lay leader said.

In the midst of his caring pastoral work, Tony "talks with people before decisions," said a lay leader. It is important, though, that he shows care, through pastoral attention and listening, and through leadership about changes, both for the ways people relate to each other and for the outcome. A significant learning from Tony's ministry is that a strong leader need not abandon either the process or the desired outcome, that both can be valued with integrity and honesty.

That strong bonds persist between Tony and the lay leaders with whom I spoke. It points to a healthy sharing of leadership, another gift he brings to situations where resistance occurs. He works in collaborative ways with lay leaders, trusting their wisdom, sharing with them the visionary tasks as well as the work of listening to resistance. Tony is very much present with all kinds of groups within the Peoples congregation, since by pastoral care he has grown into these relationships as the years have passed. He has used these years wisely and effectively, and many would say very successfully.

SEEKING ACTIVE PARTNERSHIP
Michigan Park Christian Church, Washington, D.C.
The Rev. Delores Carpenter, pastor

The Rev. Delores Carpenter has a vision of the character of the congregation she strives to build. It should be "a community of like mind and like heart." It has not always been this way in her 16 years at Michigan Park Christian Church. She was different from the pastors Michigan Park Church was accustomed to. It would have been enough that she was a woman in a world then (and still) predominantly male, for the African American clergy is even more male-dominated than that of Euro-Americans. In addition she is a full-time professor at Howard University Divinity School, a graduate seminary and an important institution of the African American church. The people of Michigan Park were unaccustomed to their pastor's holding two full-time ministerial positions, though this practice is not uncommon among African American pastors.

Delores brought a passion for worship that is spirited and praise-focused, and that tries to reflect the African American's yearning for freedom. This is far from white Disciples churches' simple, rational, and more restrained worship.

A brief glimpse at Michigan Park Christian Church's history reveals that the congregation was founded in the early part of the 20th century in another part of Washington, D.C. It was a typical small, white Protestant church that struggled to stay alive. In the late 1940s the congregation called the Rev. Arthur Azlein as pastor. Soon the church relocated from downtown to the Michigan Park area, a new middle-class neighborhood in the far northeast part of the city. Before many years white flight and a growing black middle class in the post-World War II expansion of Washington resulted in a near-total ethnic transformation of the community. Azlein was not one to run. He encouraged the congregation to stay in the neighborhood. In the last years before his retirement (he was the pastor for 43 years) the congregation became African American. Many of those constituents were content with the traditional worship described earlier. Azlein's leadership was heroic, and Michigan Park was one of the few urban white congregations in its judicatory that did not move to the suburbs. But the core character of the congregation, its traditional, white-dominated Disciples culture, would remain essentially unchanged until Delores Carpenter came as pastor.

She and lay leaders speak of three aspects of Michigan Park's life that have undergone major change in her ministry—worship, governance, and space. Change in any of these elements can result in far-reaching changes in the very nature of a congregation.

Particularly significant has been the change in worship music. The congregation developed a hymnal to include music not generally found in more traditional mainline denominational hymnals. Only recently have some denominations begun developing more inclusive hymnals and other worship resources. A well-trained staff at Michigan Park gives skilled and devoted leadership to a variety of musical genres. People who never thought themselves "choir types" are now singing their hearts out. Among the comments of lay leaders:

- "We've moved from a stilted service to a dynamic, liberating, spiritual one, from a conservative and self-contained way to a warm, outreaching stance."
- "A yearning deep within, that old 'Baptist somebody,' came out."
- "There has been more participation. The acolytes program allowed young people to take part."

Some told of resistance to these changes, making it clear that not everybody had bought into the new worship forms. The story is told of a time, before the worship style changed, when a worshiper who said "Amen" aloud and enthusiastically was asked to go elsewhere to worship. A fair number of people left Michigan Park for other congregations when the worship changes continued. Now, though, there is diversity in worship. One can clap or not, move rhythmically or not, say "Amen" or not, come forward for the altar call or not, and the community accepts all.

These changes did not come about by accident. Delores says her shared approach to leadership was at its strongest in worship planning. She develops lay partners with the conviction that a pastor is strong only when lay leaders contribute their insights, skills, and strengths to church life. Often, for her, the lay leaders identify a need to hold off on some changes that she might have been ready to make immediately. The congregation's leaders have sometimes decided not to push too hard when resistance has been particularly strong, choosing instead to enter change one step at a time.

Delores and lay leaders speak of worship as having covered the whole range of initiative and resistance levels, from 1 to 7. Important to the leadership in this area has been Delores's ability to combine courage with sensitivity to worshipers. She is the first to say that change would not have been possible had she tried to lead alone, as can be seen in lay leaders' measured approach to change.

Governance has been equally significant in Michigan Park's journey in these years. When Delores came, the congregation had a very large board with lay leaders carrying out almost all of the board's decisions. The pastor's authority was quite limited. Where Azlein had challenged the former congregation to stay, the congregation that emerged later in his tenure might not have been as willing to cede that kind of agenda-establishing authority to the pastor.

It was Delores's belief that a growing congregation needed a more centralized administration. A small pastoral church (about 125 participants) when she arrived, it more than doubled within a few years. As new people were added from backgrounds that placed less emphasis than did some traditional Disciples on the laity's exclusive authority in monetary and property matters, for example, tensions arose. Some people held, with Delores, that leadership should be shared, and that one unique role of the pastor was in day-to-day management. Others held that the pastor had her place—and that place didn't include these "business" issues.

Supported by a number of newer lay leaders, Delores proposed that the pastor become a voting member of the church board. "When she raised [the idea], the animosity that had been around was roused," said one layperson. "Much wrangling took place. But they began to see that the pastor wasn't trying to dominate." By the time this issue came up, Delores had been pastor for more than a decade. As one person said, "We trust her as pastor not to try to dominate. If we ever get another pastor, [members] may want to change back to keeping the pastor out of the congregation's business." According to some lay leaders, giving the pastor a vote on the board was not an earthshaking change, perhaps a level 4 or 5. Others, though, said that it was a transforming change that went to the very core of Michigan Park's way of ordering its life.

Some governance issues are yet to be resolved. The current board chair says that board participation is too low and that "duplication of effort and continuing lack of trust for the pastor [are] still frustrating."

Delores's approach to these concerns is to persist, work in partnership, and show members the underlying spiritual issues. She asks, about all decisions, "Is this a place where the Spirit is leading?" One of her prized initiatives has been a wide offering of Bible study opportunities for laypeople, ranging from very basic to graduate-level instruction. "The Bible classes have helped, as through them principles began to come forth about our life together," said one layperson. "Delores helps the scriptures come alive about management." Others say:

- "How can she be so loving?"
- "She'll never ask you to do more than she's doing."
- "She lets people know they can do things."
- "She is very complimentary, publicly so, about menial or big things."
- "She lets you hear about her vision any time you're around."

Delores has received a lot of criticism, not of her person, but of her policies and hopes. Yet she has been graceful in response. Important to note is the deep degree of personal trust for her, even on the part of people with whom she has disagreed. Witnessing the congregational meeting where, after years of discussion, the church constitution was amended to give her vote as well as voice, I found it evident that personal affection and trust won some support from people not sure about the policy change.

The other area of major change has been in building matters. For years lay committees managed decisions about property matters: Do we call the plumber or fix it ourselves? What color do we paint the kitchen walls? The pastor's involvement was not welcomed by some members. After all, this had been the work of the laity.

The other facilities issue was expansion. Michigan Park was built in pieces fitted together as best they could be at the time. Restrooms were not accessible to disabled people, stairways made progress slow for older people, the pastor's study was a tiny cubicle, and there was no good conference room. At least five years ago the congregation created a building fund, which has resulted in the construction and dedication of a Center for Christian Ministries. The center has new offices, an elevator to make the social hall accessible, a conference room, and bathrooms usable by all. Because Michigan Park is "landlocked"—that is, there is no space on any side of the building for major expansion—the process that led to development of this addition is of particular note. It was designed by an architect who is a congregation member. The plan was a product of a shared leadership team. The project's credibility is rooted in trust for Delores. This building is widely prized by the congregation's members. In a sense the building addition is the real *and* symbolic culmination of years of interaction between a powerful pastor who happens to be a black woman and a congregation that had already undergone massive change.

Analysis of Resistance and Response

The most volatile resistance to Delores's leadership came early in her ministry and was generated by changes in worship. For resisters these changes threatened the stability of the most important part of the congregation's life. The level of resistance is an indicator of the degree of change initiated, and these worship changes did in fact have a transforming effect. Delores and lay leaders worked hard to engage members in planning worship changes. Governance and property issues show as well that Delores practices active partnership whenever possible. Her goal is not to show resistant people that new ideas aren't just about her pushing her agenda, but to practice her belief that more people offer a richness of ideas.

Delores's response to resistance begins with her patience, which has also been a primary teaching model for the laity. Her spirituality, which takes a primary form of biblical training, has provided a solid way of building support and partnership with lay leaders. Delores's passion for "developing active partnership" among all members of Michigan Park has been a strong force (1) to hear and invite resisters to join ongoing conversations, and (2) to elicit shared problem solving and commitment to agreed-upon outcomes.

INFORMATION SHARING AND CONSENSUS BUILDING
Largo Community Church, Mitchellville, Maryland
The Rev. H. Jack Morris, pastor

Largo Commmunity Church was established in the early 1970s on the strength of a call Jack Morris experienced to step out in faith to form a congregation. He tells of having only $50 to his name when he began knocking on doors to invite people to participate. The first service was held at a senior high school in 1972 with 38 people attending. This service followed several interest meetings in which those who had responded joined in planning first steps. Its independence of any denominational connection gave this young church a degree of freedom from organizational expectations, but it highlighted the fragility of such a venture without institutional support. Largo Community Church calls itself "a nondenominational church that is interdenominational in its worship." The core purpose of the congregation is to offer busy people a saving encounter with God through a community that loves them and teaches them to love others.

A local polity much like that of Presbyterian churches was developed, absent the presbytery dimension, which gives linkage to other congregations. A trustee board was created to incorporate the church. Since then, a board of directors has been the major plenary body. It functions like a Presbyterian session, with the pastor presiding. It originates all motions, with all those that concern land transactions going to the congregation for a final decision. Many of the most important decisions have been about land.

Five years after the first worship service the group moved out of the high school to their own property. Bill, a layman, says that that decision, like Largo's whole story, "was handled with prayer." Jack Morris is a person of prayer, and he teaches the congregation to ground decisions in private and corporate prayer.

In three decades Largo Community Church's numerical growth has been striking. The congregation numbers over 1,000, with about 700 in worship regularly. New members must take part in a four-session study of the congregation's history and mission. Much of this material is taught by the pastor. The church now owns property in excess of 50 acres, with a large, attractive, and functional complex that has been developed in stages. Programs are offered for all ages, with major emphasis on community ministry with the poor and dispossessed. Jack travels to other parts of the world in mission endeavors, as Largo's reach is wide. He is a trained pastoral psychotherapist, and offers this ministry to the larger community as well.

While Largo Community Church is too large for Jack to visit in every home regularly, he is active in visitation with groups in the congregation. Whether it is a Sunday school class, a department committee, or one of the youth fellowship groups, Jack is visible in meetings and at other events. He sees this presence as a way to be the pastor in a situation where it would be impossible to visit each person or family. Lay leaders do much of the visitation in nursing homes and with shut-ins.

As Jack nears retirement, he contemplates his years at Largo and what will come later. The years and the hard work and dedicated ministry point to several ever-present dynamics, with only one transitional process dominating.

The most pivotal process was the movement to become a multiethnic congregation. Jack speaks of the time when he and the church were faced with a decision. "The church was all white, the neighborhood was changing [it is now predominantly African American], and I didn't know what to do. How can I change after all these years? My prayer was, 'Lord, whatever you dreamed this church to be, give me the grace to follow.' I released [yielded to] God to do what he intended to do here. Some whites left. The congregation has grown remarkably in numbers, and we are now more than 70 percent African American."

This multiethnic blending produced resistance from those who chose not to be part of an integrated congregation. It has led to resistance in other ways as well. Some newer black members have complained about worship style, because they wanted a more spirited experienced. Some even called for an African American pastor. But, said a black lay leader, "Jack's core convictions never wavered. Jack has since evolved into a willingness to broaden worship styles."

The overt move to become a multiethnic congregation was at an initiative level of 7, transforming. One important finding from Largo Community Church's experience is that if a congregation can work through resistance at a high level, it can learn to respond faithfully to resistance at lower levels. This truth can be seen in property decisions made later.

Property matters have also led to disputes and resistance. The new congregation moved to its first property five years after formation and soon built a frame building. Other expansions followed. Most recently 43 acres were purchased on which to build a family life center. At each step resisters have emerged, either because of the cost or the changes the new property would entail.

Jack expects resistance: "People resist and fear the unfamiliar. We fight death, don't we?" But he frequently comments, almost as a mantra, "We've got to do something about the status quo! What's the status quo? It's Latin for 'this mess we're in.'" His most frequent and dependable way to deal with this expected resistance is teaching and encouraging the congregation to move to consensus. Any time a major initiative is proposed, be it about program, property, worship, or anything else, the nature and rationale of the initiative are explained. The board of directors will not take a formal vote until, in Jack's words, "there is unity on the board." It is clear that partnership with the laity is important for decisions. But just as clear is the reality that in this congregation the pastor is the primary source of initiatives for change.

Largo Community Church is an independent congregation. Much is expected of the founding pastor—more, it appears, than would be the case in a denominationally linked congregation. There is a strong tendency to look to Jack for guidance. Lay leaders comment:

- "Jack will see needed changes. He prepares himself, the staff, board, and congregation."
- "We can move in our changes from level 1 to level 7. It just happens. Jack doesn't like forced change."
- "Jack is a visionary. He can see the hand of God in a situation."
- "Twenty years ago Jack said, 'The Lord gave me a vision of a church without walls. I will stay here and keep it on course.'"

Largo Community Church is an evangelical, nondenominational, multiethnic church in a fast-growing community. It is not a megachurch of the kind widely known these days. It does not have nonreligious "seeker services" for unchurched people. It excludes no one because of background. Jack speaks of Largo as a nonthreatening, nondenominational congregation that some have used on the way toward later reuniting with the traditions of their childhood.

Analysis of Resistance and Response

Many of the steps taken by Largo Community Church have generated resistance, even strong opposition at times. But with Jack as pastor the invitation has always been, "Let's talk." Most of the time enough talk, "bathed in prayer," has resulted in a new agreement to move on together in God's name. Jack's primary mode is gently but persistently to invite people to see the vision he and the leaders are proposing. Resistance has come mostly from those who fear moving ahead into unexplored territory. The resistance has been generated by self-interest and congregation-interest, both being factors in most individuals' resistance.

Jack uses two specific and related tools to prepare for change: information sharing and consensus building. One is struck with his commitment to imparting full information about any proposal. He will explain again and again if necessary. This sharing supports the principle of consensus building by seeking to address, quite often before they are even expressed, questions people raise that could later become major points of resistance. To identify these potential questions Jack and lay leaders listen intently. No decision is made without complete accord on the board of directors. While Jack and the board can't know if the whole congregation is united on all matters, the willingness, indeed the desire, to provide information applies to all in the congregation who will listen. When the information and decision are, for example, about a property matter and the congregation's support is essential, information and conversation will continue until all understand.

It isn't easy to categorize initiative and resistance levels in Largo Community Church. Most of the "initiative" processes of this congregation stretch over its whole lifetime. Yet the lay leader who said, about initiatives, "We can move from 1 to 7," was describing what seems the essence of the congregation's character. That is, whatever the degree of the initiative, the approach to it, of information sharing and consensus building, is much the same. There is a genuine sharing of information and decisions so that change, at whatever initiative level, is not merely accepted passively, but is freely chosen and supported by the members. With such a process resistance arises, but it is seldom of an intensity that will deter the congregation's mission.

Inclusive Pastoral Leadership
Lewinsville Presbyterian Church, McLean, Virginia
The Rev. Gary G. Pinder, pastor

A lay leader, Leah, described Lewinsville Presbyterian Church as "a work in progress." She was referring in particular to the process of developing strategies for wider engagement in mission and ministry by all in the congregation. But the phrase could well describe the more than three decades of partnership in ministry between the Rev. Gary Pinder and the people of Lewinsville.

Over the years since he came in 1968, Gary has served as associate pastor (his first call), interim pastor, co-pastor and, for over a decade, senior minister. Doug talks about Gary's long tenure: "It's a time when a mere mortal could go into autopilot. But he fears a plateau! He leads, directs, nudges us."

Though much has happened through the years of Gary's ministry at Lewinsville, he talks most eagerly about transitions that have been (and still are) occurring during his time as senior minister. These are the most pivotal for the congregation's current and coming life. Two ongoing movements stand out, a process of engaging people in small group and mutual ministries, and a commitment to moving "from doing mission projects to really being in mission," as Carol describes it.

Just defining these processes is sometimes a struggle. As the leaders view them, neither will ever be complete. They are not transitions that result from, or result in, single dramatic decisions such as relocating or staying put in the face of community change. We are seeking to reach "a level of congregational life that we haven't reached before," says Doug. Pressed, the leaders speak of a new depth of member involvement and congregational commitment to mission and ministry. In some congregations such deepening might come from an unexpected crisis and how it is faced. Sometimes the level is reached by the challenge of being a new congregation, or even the excitement of a dying congregation experiencing the miracle of rebirth. Lewinsville Presbyterian Church is not in a grave crisis. It does not face immediate decline or losses from community changes. It is a secure congregation in a stable time in its life. Giving is generous. New members continue to join. Programs involve people of all ages. Folk enjoy their life together here. Volunteer opportunities abound. Why, then, would this healthy place be grappling with a pair of processes that mean, in Leah's words, that "we are on a journey of transformation"? What's to transform, for crying out loud? Most congregations would pay dearly to be so vital!

The answer lies in part, I believe, in Lewinsville Presbyterian Church's history. Founded in 1846 with deep ties to the founders of the nation, this congregation had few really vital periods for most of its life. Thirty pastors have served during its 154 years, many of these leading in times of uncertainty and doubt as to whether the congregation would survive. Gary's has been the longest continuous pastoral service, and his own temperament, as one never fully satisfied with where he is spiritually, has had a deep impact on the congregation's life. Five years ago he challenged the session and congregation to look intensely at their life together in an initiative called Vision 2000. It was there that the groundwork was laid for the later initiatives to deepen mutual and small-group ministries and to move beyond missions to a real sense of mission. The leaders of Lewinsville Presbyterian Church know that vitality doesn't exist without ongoing transformation, and that if they do not see to this task, one day the church will die.

Gary is within five years of retirement. He is a gentle, soft-spoken leader who listens first. He is called an excellent preacher by all the lay leaders. One of Gary's great passions, says Phil, is to "leave the church with a cohesion that is not dependent on the presence and personality of a [particular] pastor."

Partnership is a dominant leadership value for Gary and for Lewinsville's leaders. He develops many of his personal action strategies around this value. Lay leaders declare, for example, that

- "This is not a one-man show."
- "Gary has an extraordinary ability to listen to everybody and to follow up if he hears dissonant voices."
- "Gary Pinder is hard to turn down."

He calls on the elders of the church, the session, for leadership in ways that use their individual skills. For example, one, an organizational consultant, is deeply engaged in designing and leading the search for a new understanding of the congregation in mission. Another with expertise in group process helps lead the small-group movement in which members are being invited to move beyond formality to closer relationships through Bible study, dialogue, and prayer. Gary saw these leaders' attributes and asked them to use their gifts for the church. He is not hesitant to invite others to do what he cannot do as well. Gary believes the congregation misses much if it leaves all the leading to the pastor.

Resistance to the two dominant emphases of Lewinsville Presbyterian Church has sprung up. At first these changes seemed simple enough, perhaps level 3 (adjusting) or 4 (redefining) initiatives. They may, however, become level 6 and even 7, for they can bring transformation. To become a congregation whose members will participate wholeheartedly in small groups can be threatening to some. As well, the movement from sponsoring outreach projects to "*being* missional" as a church is resisted by some. Some lay leaders characterize the resistance as coming from the intellectual voices in Lewinsville Presbyterian Church. It is not easy for the people of Lewinsville Church to hear the suggestion that they haven't been doing the best they could do. This congregation is located in an affluent Virginia community. Many members are middle- and upper-middle-class folk who work in professional careers as lawyers, teachers, consultants, artists, foreign service members, military officers—the list could continue. Because many of these professionals are trained always to question information and decisions, it is understandable that resistance would question new processes that may or may not work.

Further, Gary and lay leaders say, people who have developed the current ways of working are sometimes put off by the idea that a new way would be better. For example, this congregation has long offered a cafeteria of options for outreach service. From Habitat for Humanity to feeding the hungry and working with the county's big community ministry program, there are many avenues for people to extend compassion through personal service. Many members have worked hard to develop this plethora of opportunities. Some of them have difficulty with the new questions, because those questions seem to makes what they have done seem less important. Their resistance ranges from passive disengagement, levels 3 and 4, to active disengagement, level 5.

In fact, many in Lewinsville tend to say, "If it ain't broke, don't fix it." But, as Doug puts it, Gary has gotten help from Loren Mead, retired president of the Alban Institute, to "help us fix it even *if* it ain't broke." Mead has helped the session begin to understand movement from "discipleship" (being a student, follower, hearer) to "apostleship" (being a leader, teacher, giver); and in this process pastor and laity alike have found the call to the new qualities that come with the two initiatives underway.

Lewinsville Presbyterian Church *is* "a work in progress." It is, in many ways, a paradox. Here we see a large, active, financially secure congregation, loaded with signs of success, seeking to be more faithful. Leading this movement to a new tomorrow that some still think isn't needed are a pastor and his lay partners, who don't like plateaus but who love all the people in their charge. It is a fascinating study of movement and change where, some would say, it is needed least—and others would say it is most sorely needed because to settle down is to die.

Analysis of Resistance and Response

When resistance occurs, how do Gary and the lay leaders respond? Some of the lay leaders speak about Gary:

- "He listens to the dissonant voices."
- "He has a keen sense of where the consensus is."
- "There is no denial. We are led to face issues."
- "He always includes a cross-section of people in planning for changes."
- "He makes sure changes move slowly so as to include resisters where possible."

These are quite specific skills that have as their objective the inclusion of as many people as possible in the congregation's decisions and life. Gary's self-effacing temperament helps people know that he counts their opinions and feelings important, whether or not they agree with him.

Each of the two processes named can be seen as an initiative level of anywhere from 3 to 7, though it is likely that they will be experienced first at level 3, and only later at level 7. But if Lewinsville Presbyterian Church reaches "a level of congregational life that we haven't reached before," as Doug put it, a core reason will be the deep desire on the part of Gary and his lay partners to listen intently to all voices. The great skill here is in the capacity to listen genuinely while still maintaining principle and focus.

Gary's skills also include exemplifying for lay leaders the focus on inclusion. That is, his desire to be inclusive is lived out in his inviting and encouraging lay leaders to practice the very inclusiveness he lives. Lay leaders speak with enthusiasm about how he welcomes them into this community of leadership focused on inclusiveness. They practice what they proclaim.

TEACHING, PROPHETIC WITNESS, PASTORAL LISTENING
Alfred Street Baptist Church, Alexandria, Virginia
The Rev. John O. Peterson, pastor

If ever a congregation had reason to look back, it would be Alfred Street Baptist Church in Alexandria, Virginia. This congregation's history parallels the worst and best of America's story. Alfred Street Church evolved from a group of slaves who worshiped together early in the 19th century, if not before. No record exists of when and where those slaves worshiped, but according to oral tradition, this congregation was originally a slave gathering. Welton Quander, who has served on the deacon board since 1973, lives on Quander Road. His great-grandfather owned a farm for which the road was named. That man descended from slaves of George Mason, drafter of the Bill of Rights of the United States Constitution. This congregation's story also ties members to George Washington's slaves—people freed on his instruction after his death.

History suggests that these worshipers later became part of a larger community of Baptists in Alexandria, some seven miles north of the plantations where the slaves labored. In time the custom of separation dictated that Baptists in Alexandria be divided into white and black congregations. The First Baptist Church of Alexandria became the white congregation, and Alfred Street became the church of the black members.

Given such a history that began in immediate postrevolutionary America, it would surprise few to hear the stories attached to this amazing congregation. Serving as a gathering place for slaves, a station on the Underground Railroad, a center for a city's transformation—all these experiences and more have made Alfred Street Baptist Church special to its members and to the city's life.

And what about Alfred Street Baptist Church today? John O. Peterson has been pastor since 1964. He is only the fifth pastor in 197 years. His predecessor had a 38-year pastorate. Said Richard, a deacon: "This congregation treats its pastors well."

Three change processes offer a context for understanding John's leadership approach, and they tell much of the story of his pastoral ministry at this church. The first was decisions and actions related to buildings and facilities. The second was an intentional move to become an evangelizing congregation, no longer serving a traditional handful, but drawing members from the whole metropolitan Washington area. The third came some years into John's pastorate—a decision to ordain the first woman as a deacon in Alfred Street's particular Baptist association (or middle judicatory), and later to ordain a woman as a minister.

Property and space were the first major issues John had to face at Alfred Street. For many decades before his pastorate Alfred Street had occupied a historic building in downtown Alexandria. Early in John's tenure a proposal was made to raze the old building and erect a well-planned larger facility on the same site to accommodate a larger congregation, for the church had begun to grow. Some years of tension followed, both within the church and between the church and a historic-preservation interest group. In time the city bought the old property, allowing Alfred Street to build on nearby property.

It is easy to believe that a small, black congregation would be excited but also anxious about the idea of leaving a secure house of worship for something much more elaborate, perhaps even grandiose. Resistance initially focused on the idea of demolishing the old historic space. Some of this resistance was at levels 6 and 7, high enough to lead to a resolution that preserved the historic building while approving the building of a new structure. "The people just didn't understand," said one lay leader. John's primary response was to teach. He spent countless hours with groups and individuals trying to help them understand that it was neither his desire nor that of the other leaders to tear the old building down, even though the congregation required more functional and extensive space. Rather, if some solution could be found to preserve it and build as well, that would be best. (In time the city purchased the old building; it is in use today as a museum.) The teaching approach was the notable action he took.

Alfred Street Baptist Church has changed since the larger building was constructed. It is located in downtown Alexandria, now in a well-planned and functional building. On several floors, with class and conference rooms and offices, it is thoroughly accessible to disabled and elderly people. The sanctuary provides space for many people to worship, and 3,100 are active in several worship services and otherwise. When John came 36 years ago, 275 members were on the rolls, and "178 was all our clerk could find," he said, chuckling.

To understand Alfred Street's move to be evangelistic in character, we need to understand a phenomenon that has happened in increasing numbers of historically African American congregations since the civil rights movement. Many black people, empowered by that movement and its gains, yet frustrated by obstacles that have continued to stand in the way of justice, have taken strength and power from the spiritual community of the church. Throughout enslavement and the subsequent years of racism, one place where African Americans have experienced the freedom that God promises is in the church. Because of renewed appreciation for God's promises, many small, formerly maintenance-focused congregations have grown in recent decades in their sense of mission and in numbers. Some of the largest churches in many cities in the United States are African American congregations that grew from the hundreds to the thousands in the latter half of the 20th century. Alfred Street is one of these.

Alfred Street makes membership an important decision. Participation in a course of study is required of all new members. This three-month Sunday-school course addresses what it means to be a Christian, the history of the Baptist church and its conventions, and the particular ministries of Alfred Street Baptist Church.

Resistance to growth at Alfred Street was not, as might be assumed in some largely white congregations, rooted in a desire to retain the quality and size of the community. Rather, the resistance has been more related to governance. From a board of deacons of the congregation's patriarchs who *ruled*, to a younger, more flexible board, and a pastor who says, "You can't lead looking back," some black churches, including Alfred Street, have changed. The resistance at Alfred Street was found in a reluctance to yield a form of governance that gave power to older laymen. There had been some dissatisfaction with the older system, because it excluded many members from positions of authority. But the system had long been a source of stability. Changing to make governance more democratic as well as to strengthen the pastor's role in the congregation's decision making generated resistance at levels 4 and 5.

Leaders who generally appreciate John's leadership style speak of it in such terms as Welton uses: "He is a leader dedicated to the cause, with some flaws."

- *Richard*: "John is even-handed in his pastoral care, very supportive. "He leads with prayer and has the courage of his convictions."
- *William*: "John always explains to people what is being done. He does this with all age groups, even sharing information with those who oppose his ideas. He is a good administrator."

The third major time of transition at Alfred Street Baptist Church centered on the ordination of the first woman deacon and, later, the first woman minister. Within the congregation there was little resistance, but the move was not as well received in the Baptist association of which Alfred Street is a member. Because "it created an uproar in the northern Virginia area," said Richard, it resulted in criticism and some resistance within Alfred Street Church. According to Mr. Wair, John first brought it to the attention of the board of deacons, saying "that on the basis of God's giving of spiritual gifts to all who are faithful, this should have been done before."

When the association's ministerial organization objected strongly to the ordination of a woman deacon, John resigned his membership in the body, an action involving some risk because of the loss of part of his denominational support system. This experience broke ground for the ordination of a woman in ministry. Alfred Street now has a female associate minister.

For some, women's ordination seems a passé issue. In many African American traditions it remains an issue filled with stress, because though black churches may offer a strong witness about the evils of racism and other forms of social oppression, many of their internal norms and theological tenets are quite conservative with regard to women's roles in the church's vocations.

John's leadership in this issue is striking in the degree to which he was willing to stand against colleagues and the larger church. But he didn't act without considerable teaching in his own congregation about the justice of God's spiritual gifts, that they are given to all who seek God regardless of gender. According to the testimony of lay leaders, it was the teaching, as much as the courageous stand taken, that resulted in the lack of strong resistance to this transition at Alfred Street.

Bold, compassionate, determined, and always deeply faithful, John is a fascinating and strong pastor-leader.

Analysis of Resistance and Response

John cites events from his childhood, on a farm in highly segregated Virginia, that taught him about leadership. One of these lessons is that in a society that is uncertain for African Americans (and for all people of color, for that matter), one must be sure of his or her actions, confident of convictions. He also learned that "You can't lead looking back," a truism forever valid for a farmer walking behind a plow. He is still learning, he says, how to use the leadership gifts within him. In the three changes described, these gifts appear among John's actions.

Teaching. As part of the teaching team in the new-member program, John helps prepare people to live the Christian life and, in the congregation's name and interest, equips people for coming changes. He stresses the sureness of God and the need to continue growing and changing as we discern new ways to serve. John sees himself in a rabbinical role, as a teacher of teachers. Much of his teaching has been with deacons and other leaders.

Courageous prophet. John does not back off from doing and saying what he believes to be right. At times he simply believes he must hold to his conviction in the face of strong resistance, and that is all he can do.

Pastoral listening. It might seem to be a paradox that one deemed a prophet with the courage of his convictions is also a thoughtful listener. John is a pastor who takes time to listen to his people, and who believes that prophetic utterance requires hearing both God and God's people.

These three tools—teaching, being a courageous prophet, and listening pastorally—have been John's primary resources in leading change and meeting resistance to those changes. Fear of change has been a primary source of resistance. The balance of courage and empathic listening by John and lay leaders has been a response to this fear. John continues to encourage lay leaders to join him in giving bold leadership.

PURPOSE-DRIVEN AND COMPASSIONATE
Geist Christian Church, Indianapolis, Indiana
The Rev. Randall Spleth, pastor

Science is coming to understand chaos today as a process in which some of the most creative activity takes place. This is in contrast to other theories that regard chaos as a realm of utter disruption. Some scientists are developing a theory of "deterministic chaos," a state wherein all the possible movements within a system can be identified and, at least, awareness of all possible eventualities exists.

It is not so likely that all possibilities in human behavior can be mapped out, yet the contexts where those behaviors take place remain points of great creativity. Because this is true, at Geist Christian Church in Indianapolis it is said, "We thrive on chaos!" This congregation often strides off into the unpredictable, doing what few congregations have done before, risking in ways many others would fear.

It began after the Rev. Randall Spleth and his wife, the Rev. Ann Updegraff-Spleth, moved to Indianapolis in 1985, drawn there by her receiving the offer of a high-level position with one of their denomination's general offices. They would not move, however, until Randy received a similarly challenging call to ministry in Indianapolis. It came when the middle judicatory asked him to be the pastor/developer of a new congregation in a growing part of the city.

The first worship service attracted 30 participants. Growth has been strong and steady; now nearly 600 regularly attend one of the two worship services, and a third service is being planned. Not many new congregations have grown more rapidly. Other dimensions of Geist's and Randy's continuing transformations are also striking. Within months of the congregation's formation Geist began negotiating for an excellent property, which the congregation purchased at a low price. A few years later, when sanctuary plans were ready for implementation, the denomination's extension service provided the congregation with the largest financing package in this lending institution's history. Early in its life Geist Christian began a weekday children's ministry, which now serves over 300 kids a week. This "side-door" ministry has brought a number of people into the congregation. Four people from Geist Church have been called, trained, and ordained. The pastor meets regularly with 12 other people who are heeding a call to enter some form of professional ministry.

What most fully characterizes Geist Christian Church is the rapid pace of change. This rapidity grows out of the nature of Randy's leadership. He describes himself this way: "I am so entrepreneurial, it is like former football player Tony Dorsett, who would speak of seeing the hole in the line before it opens up." Lay leaders and other staff members support Randy's self-assessment.

- *Esther*: "Each building project is followed by another we couldn't afford. Otherwise, Randy says, we'd coast."
- *David*: "Randy has an enviable ability to engage us in moving in his direction and making us think we did it."
- *Todd*: "Randy uses leaders as sounding boards. How could you not come to the same conclusion [as his]?"
- *Kris* (minister of evangelism): "Randy has enough vision to exhaust us all. He gets us all caught up in it."
- *Courtney* (education director): "From the beginning Randy has had a vision for this church. He involves people in it, keeps us up to speed and more."
- *David* (music director): "In staff meetings we'll think he's 'off the wall.' His excitement is contagious."

Both lay and staff leaders describe Geist as a staff-dependent congregation. This is not to say that the gifts of laypeople are not valued. Indeed, a staff colleague spoke of Randy's "remarkable ability to see skills and opportunities for ministry beyond what the person self-envisions." One layperson said, however, that "sometimes the staff isn't as on board as Randy would be—he usually drags them along." Several, including Randy himself, have observed that, "as size grows, you lose control." This experience has not been easy for him, having himself grown in 16 years from church founder to organizer to long-tenured pastor.

Spleth's purpose-driven style of leadership has, in many ways, become that of the leadership of the congregation. As one would assume, the leadership shows strong qualities. Geist has a continuing master plan committee that has been a most important partner to Randy in putting vision into specific action steps. This committee holds much authority in the congregation, with its plans often forming, being formed by, or reinforcing Randy's vision.

One of Randy's foremost qualities is his pastoral care. Said one member: "He calls himself one of us. He comforts and challenges us this way." Not only has his family grown up with the families of the people of this young congregation, but he is indeed a compassionate person. Not all purpose-driven people are also caring about individuals. Randy combines these two gifts in great degree. Consistent with this combination is his capacity to be attentive in crises. Lay and staff leaders alike remarked on Randy's empathy and support in times of deep pain or distress.

Spiritual grounding has been an important part of Geist's life. There are weekly prayer breakfasts for men and women. Prayer is an important part of gatherings. While the fast-paced style of change and life at Geist might suggest overconfidence on the part of the pastor and others, there is, at the very least, a conscious and regular effort to remember their dependence on God and to be grateful to God for their growth.

In trying to describe the continuing changes in Geist's life, the staff and lay leaders are clear that, for example, changes in staff roles range from level 4 (redefining) to level 7 (transforming). That is to say, a staff person's initial work may be in a fairly defined and narrow program. In time, that program may take on a whole new character, and with it the staff person's responsibilities change. In the children's ministry changes are described by staff as level 5 (ongoing retooling). In evangelism, said Kris, there were 125 additions in 1999, and midway through 2,000, 53 new families had already joined. "That is a constant 7 (transforming)," Kris observed. "One-third of the congregation wasn't here this time last year."

A liability of this rapid growth has been the difficulty Geist Christian Church's leaders have had in finding reliable ways to assimilate new members into the congregation's life. Randy laments this problem. The congregation's leaders appear more focused on bringing new people in than on making them an integral part of the community once they join. When those people who are nominally involved do not then all become resisters, the fact of their moderate involvement becomes a low-level nagging reality, as though it were a type of resistance.

Analysis of Resistance and Response

Resistance to the ongoing changes in Geist Christian Church has certainly reared its head. But the resistance has been tempered by two factors. First, its being a young congregation means that many who have joined did so because they chose a young church where change would be more constant than in an older one. Second, Randy is masterful at anticipating resistance and reaching to respond before it becomes focused. He is intentional about speaking with those he believes may have the most questions. He knows the people and anticipates their questions. He does not back off for fear of difference or confrontation, though he doesn't invite it. Lay and staff leaders are learning to do this as well.

Lay and staff leaders speak of Randy's skill in this regard. One said: "He anticipates where resistance will be, how much we will tolerate. He prepares for battles very well." Another observed: "We've had unhealthy as well as healthy resistance"—that is, resistance that is simply negative, and resistance that comes from genuine care about the congregation's direction. The latter kind, caring resistance, is normally practiced by people who are willing to enter the ongoing conversation about where the congregation is headed.

Such strategies as the master plan committee, said one lay leader, "are ways to deal with resistance." Randy is most willing to incorporate the best ideas of the resisting ones and to give them credit. He talks with key people in the church, gets the facts, and will take risks to hear. Because Geist Christian Church is in a continuing process of transformation, none of the initiatives would be at any point below the 5-to-7 range.

Certainly challenges face Geist Christian Church. The rapid growth has not always allowed time to train new members in discipleship. This failing has resulted in what Randy himself calls a congregation of "Sunday-morning Christians." Related to this phenomenon is the staff dependence referred to earlier, along with a sense that many newer members who were previously unchurched have not become even nominal, much less strong financial stewards. A personal dilemma for some lay leaders is the reality that "some are intimidated by [Randy] and won't tell him if they disagree." Another challenge is the assimilation of new people. "The infrastructure [to assimilate] is not there." A consequence is what one leader called a "revolving door" of people in and out. This latter concern is not widespread. Many stay. But the rapid changes mean that new people do not become involved as rapidly as would be desired. It is a circular dilemma, for the very rapidity of growth and change that has been Geist's strength has not allowed Geist the time to develop ways to engage all the new people deeply to tap into their strongest gifts. And this rapidity of growth has also kept some resistance from being identified or expressed, as some members have simply not had time to become engaged to the point that they have felt they could name their resistance. Thus one area of concern is that this high proportion of unassimilated members can result in a lack of support for changes.

Nonetheless, Geist Christian Church is a remarkable and exciting place to be these days, perhaps as close as we can come to a denominationally loyal prototype of the emerging congregation of the new age.

Conclusion

This journey to eight congregations offers us food for reflection about congregational life and, in particular, the ways pastors and other leaders initiate change and respond to resistance. Resistance can always be expected in a system where change is taking place. For it to not happen would require that a congregation have no people.

FOR REFLECTION

In chapter six you will see a case study model, which I suggest be used to look at your own congregation. Look at it, but for now reflect on these initial qualities.

1. Would you describe the leadership approach in your congregation as telling, selling, facilitating, collaborating, or a blend of these? Why?

2. What issues have generated changes in your congregation?

3. At what "degree" would you place these changes?

4. Have these changes resulted in resistance? If so, what forms did the resistance take?

5. How did the pastor and other leaders respond to the resistance?

CHAPTER 4

Responding to Resistance

In this chapter I examine the ways leaders in the eight congregations respond to resistance. These congregations are all flawed. They could not be otherwise. Perhaps in my descriptions they sound like perfect places. Not so. After many years of coaching and consulting with congregations of many shapes and sizes, I know how very small (I don't mean in size) they can be. The exciting part of examining congregations so closely is to see how powerfully God's presence can be felt, even amid all the flaws. Just as roses have both flowers and thorns on the same stems, so congregations of grace have deep flaws. I am not in search of the perfect parish so much as of parishes where the people of God reach through and despite their imperfections to seek God's guidance. I find this grasping for God's guidance to be a quality of these eight congregations, and I believe it is possible in *all*.

For reference, here is the chart from chapter 2 that describes resistance levels.

Figure 8
Levels of resistance in congregational life

Resistance	Initiative	Passive/ Active	Range of behavioral responses in resistance	Hoped-for benefits
L1	Maintaining	Passive	Apathy	Valuing an important program
L2	Reinforcing	Passive/ active	Apathy; questioning	Cooperating to strengthen good parts of a congregation's life
L3	Adjusting	Passive & active	Passive disengagement to limited cooperation	Partnership to identify and address needed adjustments
L4	Redefining	Passive & Active	Withdrawing, friendly questioning	Congregation cooperating in craft identity
L5	Retoolng	Passive & active	Loyal opposition, willingness to compromise	Sharing, discerning new forms of action together
L6	Restructuring	Active doubled	Loyal opposition, active disengagement/ "wait it out"	Deep mutual understanding & work to find new directions
L7	Transforming	ACTIVE	Loyal oposition, threatened or real departure	Working, risking, daring to disagree, trust grows

New Congregations
Largo Community Church and Geist Christian Church

Largo Community Church and Geist Christian Church are young congregations. The current pastors, the Rev. Jack Morris and the Rev. Randall Spleth respectively, were the founding pastors. They and the congregations have grown and changed together. One life-cycle model theorizes that a congregation goes through five stages: formation, expansion, stabilization, breakdown, and crisis.[1] Both these congregations stand with one foot in expansion and the other in stabilization. Expansion is that time when a congregation is growing to its stable size. When it reaches that size, the congregation, still remembering its founding dream, is most productive without feeling stresses of decline and shortage of resources like money and leadership. The lives of these two congregations have been taken up with the hard work of growing, and that includes productive and painful work.

Both congregations have reached out in particular to people who had no church affiliation. Some of these new members had turned away from the congregations of their youth and hadn't been in church since. Others had never been churchgoers. Thus they didn't bring recent experiences with other churches to Largo and Geist.

Resistance, therefore, came less from folk who claimed to know what they were doing or who were yearning for the good old days than from people adjusting to new directions. This was level 4 resistance, with cooperation being the positive outcome. Many people in new congregations are there in part because they were looking for a pioneering place. Not always wedded to traditions, they want to help shape new communities. Sometimes, however, new congregations are begun by groups who have left existing churches. If they come from more than one congregation, resistance can sometimes arise when some people do things the way they were done in another congregation and others resist. This resistance can be level 5 or even 6, seeking new direction together, but sometimes leaders encounter disengagement if resisters feel disenfranchised. People might also resist because they are "doing battle" with a previous congregation: "I'll make sure this pastor doesn't do X, as Pastor Last did!" This is level 6 and 7 resistance. We can see that in a new congregation most resistance comes from two groups: those who bring histories from prior congregational experiences and want either to replicate or to resist that history, and those with little or no congregational experience who may resist change that they don't understand in the new congregation. In Geist and Largo less resistance stemmed from other congregations' imported ways than from people learning a new kind of community.

LONG-LIVED AFRICAN AMERICAN CONGREGATIONS
Alfred Street Baptist Church and Peoples Congregational UCC

Alfred Street Baptist Church and Peoples Congregational UCC are African American congregations with long, rich histories. Both have experienced the life cycle described above more than once. Before Tony Stanley was called as pastor, Peoples Congregational had, for some years, enjoyed a stable period. But at the end of the predecessor's very long pastorate, a time of uncertainty had preceded Tony's call. Alfred Street, however, had been in a decline when John Peterson came. Now, a third of a century later, both congregations have undergone striking transformations and are again stable. Both pastors have served for more than three decades, keeping fresh and renewed, and both congregations have lay leaders who gladly work with the pastors, continuing to discover the excitement of partnership.

Soon after Stanley and Peterson arrived in these congregations, significant changes took place. The pastors' leadership and that of lay leaders were tested. In both cases long-time members felt vulnerable when a place where they had felt safe began to change. At Alfred Street Baptist the change focused on a historic building and the need for new and better facilities for the growing congregation. Peoples Congregational faced an important change in constituency as younger professional people came in growing numbers, their presence often seeming to push older members into more obscure roles.

In both cases the resistance came from established constituencies. At Alfred Street people questioned abandoning their historic building. Some members were from families whose ancestors had built that very building. At that early point in Peterson's pastorate members also voiced apprehension of and resistance to the cost of this change, reaching levels 4 and 5. Members of the opposition were not at the point of walking out but remained loyal, even as they questioned the proposed property change. Most of the people had had to scrape, in a Jim Crow world, for what they had. Money came hard, and they were suspicious of parting with it too easily. For many the church had been the only public place where they were free.

Resisting change was, for them, an acknowledgment of their feelings of vulnerability.

Peoples Congregational had been supported and guided for decades by people who were now feeling less important in the congregation's life than before. Those raising questions were veterans of the congregation whose love of the church was beyond question. They had supported the church through times of racism and thus peril for African Americans. For some, though they welcomed the changes that finally came with civil rights laws, the overt appeal to a younger constituency made it seem as though their long-suffering and courage were being given short shrift. It was a complex kind of resistance, still level 5, sometimes level 6, for there was some disengagement and inactivity; but this resistance was not used to threaten. While long-time members knew that new and young people were needed, these new members were not always offered a comfortable welcome.

Old Congregations in Renewal
Pilgrim Congregational UCC and First Christian Church, Frankfort

According to the life-cycle model discussed earlier (formation, expansion, stabilization, breakdown, crisis), these two congregations were in decline when their current pastors began their ministries.

First Christian Church, Frankfort, Kentucky, was in decline, but not far enough into "breakdown" for a major sense of urgency to prevail. The parish had undergone a peaceful interim ministry and a placid process of searching for a new pastor. This period lasted about 15 months. No major disruptions occurred, and the church was ready for the new pastor's leadership (or so members thought).

After Gary Straub had been there for a while, some members wondered if indeed they were ready. Both supporters and resisters of the congregation's new direction raised questions. Gary's patient style, in which his commitment to needed changes was clear but not radical enough to scare people, was good for this congregation. In time, though, as some people saw the level of decline and began to perceive the depth of change taking place, resistance began to show its face. Resistance appeared at levels 4 and 5—active, but not severe enough to result in resisters leaving the congregation. Much of this resistance, said lay leaders, came from people who were proud of First Christian's story, some of whom felt attacked when their way of doing things was questioned. The question facing Gary and lay leaders was how to affirm the love these people had for the church while also helping them join the growing consensus for change.

Pilgrim Congregational Church, Cleveland, Ohio, was nearing the end of its life. That the interim ministry and search process lasted 10 years may be a record, at least for that area of the denomination. The symbolic power of restoring the pipe organ helps us understand the resistance at Pilgrim. Some of it came from people too tired of trying to keep their church alive to do any more than resist. For 20 years they had worshiped without their grand pipe organ. A sense of helplessness to fix either the organ or their life as a congregation had them in its spell. Such resistance was level 1 or 2, marked by apathy. The Rev. Laurie Hafner's decision to press on with the organ reconditioning and repair, even though it was costly and some people did not support the effort, was appropriate, and her taking the risk that this might become an important symbol for a new day paid off.

In addition, resistance was encountered because proposed change brought into question long-standing values of the congregation. The year-long study process on human sexuality evoked resistance from some. It ranged from levels 3 and 4, as some chose to stay away, to levels 6 or 7, or active opposition to change. The inclusive nature of the study did more than blunt this resistance, however. It actively engaged those willing to take part. In time some resisters began to lend their energy to the process and, later, to implementing the decision to become an Open and Affirming congregation.

From Pilgrim, we learn that both the resistance that comes from extreme fatigue and that which comes from a willingness to die for our values can occur in a congregation in severe decline. As always, the question is not how to get rid of the resistance but how to listen to it and work with it for the sake of the church.

From First Christian, Frankfort, we see that when resistance to significant change emerges in a congregation soon after what many consider its best days, resisters might be especially eager to get back to what worked. Because some of what worked may yet be the better way for some things to be done, this resistance needs to be heard and those expressing it invited to contribute to real problem-solving.

AN URBAN TRANSITION CONGREGATION
Michigan Park Christian Church

Michigan Park Christian Church in Washington, D.C., unlike First Christian, Frankfort, and Pilgrim Congregational, was not in a decline when it underwent the changes recounted here. And unlike Peoples Congregational and Alfred Street Baptist, it is not a historically African American congregation. Michigan Park, like a cat, has lived more than one life. It is in at least its fourth. The first life was lived in another location as a family church. The second life began with the move to the present site, followed by expansion for a couple of decades, until racial and ethnic change came. The change brought new stability, though membership declined slightly. Uncertainty about the future followed the retirement of the pastor who had led the church through that change. The 15-year pastorate of the Rev. Delores Carpenter has resulted in new expansion. There are, however, many signs that a period of stabilization has begun.

Michigan Park is a blend of veteran members, many of whom preceded Carpenter's arrival and have a history with the denomination, and newer people, many of whom were attracted not by the denomination, but by the pastor, friends, family, the church's location, or its program. The latter motivation is quite typical of people who enter many churches these days, with denominational loyalty playing a decreasing role in their choice.

Some of the tensions that have arisen in the congregation, notably from changes in worship and governance, have thrust into conflict people with long denominational histories and those without. Those new to the denomination have often been the most supportive of changes identified with Delores.

When change began taking place in worship, resistance was dramatic, certainly at levels 6 and 7. Not only did transformation occur in the congregation's worship life, but those who could not deal with the change either refused to be involved or left the congregation. Few of those still active are now resistant to the spirited worship of Michigan Park. This worship style speaks eloquently to the struggle for freedom that has been the story of African American people. It is understandable that many of those whose prior worship style had been more sedate could embrace the new way warmly. Many black people are still not that far from a time of subjugation when worship was literally the only arena where their God-given freedom could be celebrated.

Resistance to changes in governance has not been as severe. Though some of it came from the same sources as resistance to the worship changes, it was more of a level 5 resistance, with a loyal opposition willing to compromise and reach understandings in the best interest of the congregation as a whole. For some, that compromise came from trust in Delores, though some have suggested that dissenters hold out the option of reverting to exclusion of the pastor from governance after the current pastor's tenure ends.

A STRONG SUBURBAN CONGREGATION
Lewinsville Presbyterian Church

Lewinsville Presbyterian Church, McLean, Virginia, is strong and stable, though life has not always been easy for the congregation. Because we tend to see ourselves only as we are now, we may need to be reminded what brought us to this point. This church was founded in a rural area, and it must often have been difficult to find pastors willing to travel eight to 10 miles out of the city to preach and celebrate the sacraments in the tiny congregation. Lewinsville's current several hundred active members, its lovely and practical building, and its strong staff and high-quality program seem to place it light years from that history.

It is this strength and stability that provide both the blessing and the challenge for Lewinsville's pastor and lay leaders. The Rev. Gary Pinder is not one to be satisfied with the status quo. He tries to help leaders see that an apparently prosperous period can be tricky, because members may be tempted to come to rest and enjoy our prosperity forever. Yet such satisfaction is a guaranteed route to decline and eventual death. It is likely that Lewinsville has never before enjoyed such an apparently stable time, so it seems natural that members want to hold on to this comfort however they can.

The changes underway are intended to deepen the commitment of members to each other in supportive ministries and to enable the congregation to come to an identity as mission-centered and reaching out in all that it does. Servanthood is the new key element in this process of change. This, in the perceptions of leaders, contrasts with a past and present of great dependence on the pastor for supportive ministry, and a programmatic approach to outreach that invites people to be involved if they so choose.

Resistance to the changes at Lewinsville Presbyterian Church has come largely from people who are quite happy with things as they are. It would be understandable for the congregation to focus primarily on maintenance of the current health and vitality. But vitality by definition suggests life and change, and leaders who advocate change appear more in touch with the need for change than are those who opt for maintenance. Thus resistance has its source in people who believe that their church needs no change. Because the changes encouraged by leaders begin as redefining efforts and move to a higher level, the resistance at this time appears to be level 5, with a loyal opposition that is willing to share its concerns and even compromise, working within the congregation's process.

WAYS OF RESPONDING TO RESISTANCE

A close look at these eight congregations discloses two kinds of positive responses to resistance. By positive I mean receptive, with openness to hearing resistance. One of these responses is what can be called, borrowing a medical term, "pre-existing conditions." These qualities and behavior patterns are in place before resistance appears, and enhance the congregation's whole life. The second kind of response is directed at the particular resistance. This kind of response is focused on each occurrence of resistance, yet it requires certain skills on the part of leaders. This kind of response depends largely on the actions of leaders, while the first is a response of the congregation as a whole.

Five organizational qualities appear particularly important in the congregation's capacity to receive and respond appropriately to resistance. These qualities make the congregation better able to carry out its mission and ministry—less defensive, more open in its organizational processes, and more likely to consider how new ways of doing things can be helpful. These qualities need to be built into the congregation's culture, for they cannot just be revved up to meet whatever resistance might arise in the face of a particular initiative. They are not qualities that can be created in a crisis, nor are they qualities that exist only to respond to resistance. They undergird healthy growth and change. They enhance the congregation's faithful obedience to God. They are also significant tools in responding to resistance, and this is, in a sense, a bonus.

I saw varying degrees of all five qualities in each of the congregations. The five qualities are

- A context of trust
- Shared leadership
- Vision and the passion to share that vision
- Spiritual discipline
- Systems awareness, including understanding of and openness to change

I will cite various examples of these from the eight congregations studied.

A Context of Mutual Trust

Trust—a willingness to place oneself another's hands—is basic to the health of a congregation. Pastors and other leaders gain the confidence of members by their trustworthiness. But trust must run two ways. It is just as important for a congregation's leaders to trust members as it is for those leaders to be trustable.

A context of mutual trust is essential if resistance is going to be willingly expressed and received. No matter how much a resister may disagree with a leadership initiative, if he doesn't have some trust in the leader, he will be less likely to offer resistance openly. And no matter how skilled a leader is at proposing initiatives, if she doesn't have enough trust in the congregation at least to listen to resistance, the congregation's decision-making processes will appear to be closed.

Jack Gibb, a social psychologist with years of experience in analyzing trust development in groups, says that trust development has four stages: data-flow, acceptance, control and decision-making.[2]

- *Data-flow* means mutual sharing of information so that each participant knows that he or she is heard and hears others.
- *Acceptance* is the sense that one is now a member of the group, for not only is one heard and hearing others, but is accepted by, and accepts, others.
- *Control* is the group's capacity to decide and accept whoever is leading and the norms and values by which leadership will be carried out.
- *Decision-making* is now possible, because the group has moved in its trust beyond competition about leadership and the use of power.

Three principles underlie the progression of these stages:

1. When breakdown occurs at any stage, it is necessary to return to the previous stage and to do that stage's work again. If people are not finding acceptance, it means that data-flow is not taking place as it could.
2. A group must continually examine its life through all the stages, for to assume that once a group is able to make decisions it will never need to return to control (or even to data-flow and acceptance) is a mistake.
3. A healthy group will seek and find a balance wherein the members will give appropriate attention to seeing to the health of relationships as well as the tasks at hand. It is easy for congregations to become so task-oriented that little time is spent in maintaining health. Some questions can help this maintenance work:

- Are we listening to each other?
- Do we allow people to finish what they are saying, or do we cut them off?
- Do some of us dominate conversations?
- Do we regularly ask each other how we are feeling about the group?

It is critical for leaders of congregations to pay attention to maintenance of healthy interaction so that groups can do their work well. Relationships among and between individuals and groups are the most basic places where we experience systemic interplay. If these are cared for regularly, and not put off until things fall apart, the congregation can be a trusting place.

Pilgrim Congregational United Church of Christ is a congregation whose pastor has taught trust by demonstrating it. Leaders were impressed by Laurie Hafner's willingness to trust people who resisted the Open and Affirming study process. She wanted the church to be inclusive of them as well as of gay and lesbian people. Yet it was a powerful risk to be so welcoming of those outsiders, for at any time a strong resister could have raised "such a ruckus," as one person said, that the whole process might have been derailed. She trusted the resisters and those already supportive of being Open and Affirming, and she trusted herself. In this way she warranted the trust of both supporters and resisters so that all could be mutually open and honest.

From the start of his pastorate at First Christian Church, Frankfort, Gary Straub stressed the importance of mutual trust among leaders. In regular meetings of the elders, time is taken for prayer, concerns of the congregation, leadership issues, and the maintenance of the group's own health. Eight years into his pastorate, I observed Gary and an elder of the congregation leading a daylong retreat for 150 elders from 25 other congregations. The most compelling feature of that event was the way Gary and his co-leader trusted each other and shared leadership fully. Because Gary and his fellow leaders appeared relaxed, open, and eager to hear from those with different perspectives, it all looked very easy. As one leader said, "It appears that all you have to do is be laid-back." It isn't easy. A leader's learning to be a nonanxious presence is essential for a social system's health. This trusting manner allows the expression of resistance.

At Lewinsville Presbyterian Church all decisions about congregational directions are made by the leadership team. Gary Pinder takes seriously his role as teaching elder, and all other elders are challenged to take their leadership just as seriously. At its annual retreat the session attends to its health as a group as well as its shared leadership responsibilities. I was guest leader for that retreat one year, using as the major content the Myers-Briggs Type Indicator (an inventory of personality types based on Swiss psychologist Karl Jung's findings.) Of equal importance were participants' individual typologies and how they could as individuals best serve the congregation, and the ways their self-knowledge could be used to make their shared leadership as vital as possible. Among the lessons learned was the importance of hearing differences, even resistance, within the session itself. This awareness has helped the elders to be increasingly open and responsive to resistance from the congregation.

It is reasonable, I believe, to say that the development of a growing community of trust must undergird all other pre-existing conditions if a congregation is going to be a constructive place to express and hear resistance.

Shared Leadership

One of the very encouraging factors in all of the congregations I studied is the high value placed on shared leadership. Responses of lay leaders showed a strong commitment on the part of all pastors to shared leadership. In general, I find that some clergy work toward shared leadership because it is an expected and necessary part of effective congregational life, while some clergy don't place much value in it.

In these congregations the pastors not only know the necessity of good lay leadership; they enjoy working in such a partnership. They seek to develop leaders' skills. They believe that good leadership in congregations is crafted and shaped with good leader-development strategies. Wise clergy don't assume that shared leadership will come into existence by some mysterious power. Nor do they think that, once developed, it will remain standing on its own power. These pastors work at it, revising their ways of training leaders and growing new leadership all the time, with particular emphasis on enabling the spiritual gifts of laypeople to be used as God wants them used. This practice isn't just a matter of expedience. Its roots are in the faith tradition that the ministry of the church is shared, not limited to just one or a few.

At Michigan Park Christian Church shared leadership can be seen in the team planning strategy that Delores Carpenter has used throughout her ministry. This approach to leadership is valuable for two reasons: more creativity is evoked when more people are engaged in a task, and the power of a team is greater than the power of one person when times of change and decision arrive. Furthermore, this shared approach can incorporate people of strong opinions who might otherwise resist, or even become hostile, if not given a voice in the conversation. It is important to note that Michigan Park doesn't practice this kind of openness in order to cut resistance off at the pass, but because various viewpoints are valued.

The shared leadership approach at Lewinsville Presbyterian Church has, as one of its objectives, identifying and evoking the gifts of the laity. In some congregations the source of resistance is people who feel they aren't called on to serve. The Lewinsville leadership makes the invitation to use gifts in the church's ministry open to all members. This open invitation has grown throughout Gary Pinder's pastorate. In addition, the congregation has, for several years, engaged in active strategic planning. As a fresh mission and goals have come forth, people who have participated in shaping these directions feel called to serve as the congregation carries out the mission. Thus an ongoing process of new congregational emphases matching newly discovered personal gifts has taken place, guided by the pastor and lay leaders. The open invitation is at the center. Gary Pinder has cultivated this sharing of leadership for years, and the leadership has caught it.

From the beginning Largo Community Church relied on team decision-making. Pastor Jack Morris knew that the new start would never take without this collective approach. Even the date of the first worship service was set by a team of interested people. Jack knows also that the strength of a decision depends on the breadth of the community that makes it. Consensus is the rule at Largo, and the leadership team makes all decisions this way. For example, when the congregation decided to purchase land or to erect a new building, the leadership team did not proceed until all agreed. Though such a process can be time-consuming, it certainly offers a way to engage resistance constructively, without being given labels that may make those who hold different points of view feel belittled or devalued. Paul's word about doing all things "decently and in order" (1 Cor. 14:40) is important to this congregation.

The importance of shared leadership in all dimensions of the congregation's life cannot be overemphasized. When resistance comes on the scene, it is too late to cook up a genuine shared approach to congregational life. The descriptions given here show unique ways in which shared leadership provides a healthy climate for responding to resistance, even before it is named "resistance."

Vision and Teaching the Vision

There is a kind of holy momentum at work in any congregation that becomes engaged in a new sense of its mission, a vision that claims its energy and talent. Robert Ceuni, the pastor of a large midwestern congregation who studied 50 large congregations, says that all vital congregations have a vision:

> As the vision takes shape, determination builds. Energy erodes malaise. Clarity about direction replaces vague disease. The emerging common vision begins to pull people out of the morass of bickering by challenging them to do more than work on their personal agendas. An enthusiastically accepted vision begins to renew spiritual health.[3]

This description of the power of a vision focuses on the development of a shared commitment to the congregation's call.

A vision is God's unique call to a congregation, and one of the tasks of leaders is to try to capture that vision in ways people can understand, so that it changes the congregation's very life. How might this happen?

Where does a congregation's vision begin? How does it become known? The churches I looked into all have a strong vision of the mission to which they believe God has called them. The vision comes from God, and the leaders are the ones who seek to put it into words that touch the lives of the people.

At Geist Christian Church one senses, from the expressions of lay and staff leaders, that Randy Spleth is always a step in front of other leaders in seeing that vision and challenging others to share it. He does not negate the roles of others. On the contrary, he seeks to engage others in the vision. Leaders trust him to see the larger picture, however, and though some people become frustrated with the rapidity of change, leaders nearly always become partners in the congregation's changes.

Not everyone in the congregation follows so readily. Indeed, some simply go to worship but have little involvement in the rest of congregational life. But a critical mass of leaders and members share the vision, giving enough support that the vision come to its feet and walks, a step at a time. All have at least an invitation and the opportunity to join the core, and many do. One possible drawback at Geist is the gap that is left between those who are on board and a good number of folk identified by Randy himself as "Sunday-only Christians." Is theirs a passive kind of resistance? In some cases perhaps, but in most it is probably just passivity. Resistance might be more desirable, because resistance would at least demonstrate a level of engagement.

Alfred Street Baptist Church had been sitting still for years. The "marriage" of Pastor John Peterson and the congregation resulted in early changes. A vision came alive, bringing together the new pastor's conviction for evangelism, the readiness of the congregation for renewal, and the historical reality that African American congregations offer a stable community for people living with the ambiguity of social change and continuing racism. John gave voice to this vision, and was supported all the way by the key leadership team of the congregation, the board of deacons. Wisely, he didn't walk out on this limb of growth and change alone. Fear was not what prevented him from acting alone, for John's faith is such that he fears very little. Rather, it was the good judgment to know that partnership with lay leaders is important both to making good decisions and to engaging any who might have a different point of view. People who resist change do not always find a welcome venue in strongly pastor-centered congregations, which is often the case in African American churches. But John

Peterson is democratic and certainly a Christian, always open to others' perspectives, so resistance has been heard.

When Tony Stanley was called to Peoples Congregational UCC, the congregation didn't realize that it was on the brink of a major change in constituency and character. A historically African American congregation in a major city, Peoples Church stood to gain from the new interest of people of color in the church. It didn't take long for Stanley and his lay partners in leadership to realize that the congregation could opt to focus on preserving its traditional membership of older, often heroic people, or welcome the newer, younger seekers. The latter became their collective vision, nurtured and shepherded by the pastor but agreed on by the congregation's leaders. Resistance came, and the response of Pastor Stanley and the lay leaders was to respect the resisters but not always to agree with their opinions. In time the urgency of sharing the gospel with younger people was persuasive, and most who may have felt pushed around by this decision accepted the validity of the new direction.

Spiritual Formation

In the eight congregations examined, spiritual formation is essential both for the clergy's own sustenance and for keeping central the church's very meaning. It is also vital as the pastor and other leaders build a community of people who share vision, mission, and strategies for congregational development.

These pastors attend to the spiritual formation of the congregation and its leaders because to do so is a part of their calling, and because they believe nothing good can be accomplished in the church without it. Who are we if not a spiritual people, founded on God's love and grace as known in Christ, and seeking to base everything we do on that truth?

Spiritual people are open to that which is beyond our own conscious resources to receive insight, strength, and motivation. Spirituality is the discipline of listening to the voice of God, which can come to us in an infinite number of ways. Spiritual formation is the process of learning to listen, including learning and practicing disciplines that enable us to hear God's "voice," so that our lives will be lived differently as a result of God's effect on us. Calling the congregation to spiritual growth means making prayer, theological reflection, and other practices part of the ongoing life of the congregation. Church-renewal and revitalization specialist Charles Olsen talks about church boards and spirituality.

> The individual board member is not to see her- or himself as merely a program manager serving the pastoral CEO or as a political representative of other interests, but as a spiritual leader with gifts and power to act. The collective body is not to see itself as a coordinating cabinet or an advisory group but as the people of God in community. The group is the body of Christ, with members having various gifts, wisdom and functions. As such the group's life is formed by scripture, prayer, silent waiting, witnessing, and serving.[4]

This description may seem to be oversimplified, but I believe it shows the approaches used by the pastors and lay leaders in these eight congregations.

At times, when listening to the people of Geist Christian Church, one wonders if there's time to practice spiritual disciplines. Matters move at what seems a frantic pace. However, this pace is undergirded by weekly prayer breakfasts for members. This congregation does not emphasize structured fellowship and service groups for men and women as in many more traditional congregations. But these breakfasts offer times for prayer and conversation, and the conversations are a time to share insights that may come from praying together. In addition to these breakfasts, say the lay leaders, the practice of prayer has been "foundational from the start." Pastor Randy Spleth models it in his life, and all events are centered in prayer for guidance and the grace to undertake emerging tasks in ways different from what we may have hoped for. Whether this approach to spirituality has a direct effect on people who might offer resistance to the congregation's decisions and directions is less clear than the simple truth that it does strengthen clergy and lay leaders to do what they believe to be God's call. This strength alone can persuade leaders to be more open in responding to resistance. Further, in any conversation with one who is resisting, the leaders begin with prayer, thus offering the possibility that God's voice may be heard in the resistance offered.

At Largo Community Church a lay leader spoke of leadership decisions all being "bathed in prayer." Pastor Jack Morris tells of the time when, in prayer, he asked God to do what must be done in regard to reaching out to minister to African Americans. The result is a congregation, more than 70 percent of whose members are people of color, and a community culture that seeks to reflect this multiethnic makeup. What is key for Largo Church is the place of prayer in its common life and in individuals' lives. From the beginning Jack taught, more by example than otherwise, about the importance of prayer. No decisions are made without prayer. The intent is not just to pray as a ritual, but to remind the community through prayer, again and again, that it is God's will, not ours, that we do. The discipline of prayer is practiced, encouraged, and taught. When people pray together, differences of opinion can be defused, or new options opened. I don't mean that prayer is used at Largo to manipulate people who might resist a decision. But as practiced, it is a call to all in the congregation to place their own opinions on hold as they seek to discern what God desires. So as prayer leads them to get out of the way so that God can prevail, it can bring to the group's awareness some opinions that may not be accurate, as well as show different points of view. Perhaps praying together cuts off dialogue. More likely, though, it opens the door for people to discuss those points of view with less determination to defend them at all costs.

First Christian Church, Frankfort, shows another method of spiritual formation. Here, early in his ministry, the Rev. Gary Straub began working with elders, one of the central lay leader groups, to develop what he has called the elders' circle. Not only do the elders pray in a more traditional way together, but they also learn other spiritual disciplines, such as centering prayer, dialogue that enhances trust development, "journaling," and biblically centered meditation. Some of these disciplines are silence-based, on the assumption that it is when we are silent that we can hear what cannot be heard when we are speaking. The effect of this ongoing training with the elders has been to form them into a community of leaders who listen not only to God, but also to other people in the congregation. I found these leaders to be among the most sensitive I have known to the feelings and opinions of others. This sensitivity certainly equips these leaders well for their responsibility to hear resistance and to give it a voice, rather than attacking it or, worse, ignoring it. Listening to God helps us listen to one another.

Tolerance for Change as Part of Systems Awareness

Strong leaders know not only that congregational change happens, but also that it is part of the congregation as a system always in movement. We don't always take easily to change. Though change happens, there is often a degree of resistance to it by many congregation members. Some cast it as something to be feared and fought.

The wondrous irony of systems is that to live, they must undergo change. Yet still they resist change. Systems seek stability and balance. Change disrupts such a state. Leaders need to know that systemic reality includes change. As we've said, change, along with other parts of life, happens, whether we plan for and welcome it or not. Buildings, equipment, people, and programs show wear, and we'd rather this aging process not happen. Sometimes we think we are settling into a "no change" mode, and it is as though one side of us believes there will be no change. Congregations can fall for the illusion that things don't change. We who work in the church may become convinced that there indeed *are* some congregations where nothing changes. We're wrong. The stories of the eight congregations show leaders with a good understanding of systems, particularly their tendency to stabilize despite the continuing reality of change.

Their leaders appreciate the value of a system's equilibrium, the anxiety that comes when that state is destabilized, yet the necessity for equilibrium and destabilization to live in a healthy tension. Though these congregational leaders may not always be able, or choose, to put the dynamics of a system's tension in these words, they place value on their congregations being open systems. That is, they want their congregations to interact with the world around them and thus be open to changes that can happen to that tension between equilibrium (stability) and destabilization.

Establishing a continuing long-range planning process early in his pastorate at Peoples Congregational Church was more important than even Tony Stanley realized. Just having such a process was different, and the fact that it was ongoing made it unique. This process has given birth to property and programmatic changes, all developed in light of the congregation's ongoing mission. Through this process the people have come to know that their congregation is not a closed, self-contained organization, accountable to no one but themselves, existing only to serve its membership. Because periodically members assess the community's needs and their gifts and potential, they are able to respond to the external world in a planned and relevant way. The congregation's approach to planning has incorpo-rated a variety of viewpoints by engaging people from various groups. The leaders understand clearly that their congregation is made up of many people and groups, and members must attend to an assortment of essential tasks such as decision-making, administration, communication, and planning. While they may not know their congregation as a "system," the leaders with whom I talked are savvy about what systems mean. This awareness and the re-sulting invitation to members and neighbors to have a voice in the planning process is one of Peoples' ways of recognizing the importance of different opinions. Without this openness, resistance could be far more intense. As it is, resistance is not ignored. Rather, anyone with a different point of view is made to feel as welcome as are the most ardent advocates of the con-gregation's programs.

Alfred Street Baptist Church sees its identity as part of a story that is over two centuries old and will outlive present members. Like a family, a congregation passes strengths and weaknesses from one generation to an-other. Alfred Street today does not want to forget the determination of a handful of slaves to worship in freedom. In this spirit John Peterson and the lay leaders sought to retain the most visible sign of their history—their build-ing—and also to go on to write a new chapter. In a system, varied parts, including dimensions of the past, present, and future, come together. In taking steps to preserve the historic structure while building for the future, engage in evangelism for a new time, and ordain the first woman deacon and the first woman minister, Alfred Street sought to link its history with today and tomorrow. In the process those who held different opinions were invited to be part of the system's life. Not all accepted the invitation, and pockets of resistance endured. John and other leaders took an open stance toward those with different opinions. Some left the church, but new people came. The importance of being true to their story remains central today for the leaders of Alfred Street. A healthy system accepts its story; it acknowl-edges its links to its past.

The first important change at Pilgrim Congregational Church after the decision to call the Rev. Laurie Hafner as pastor was to renovate the organ that had not been used for 20 years. It cost some money, but the project was achievable. More than that, it became a symbol of other new things that could happen. In a powerful way, the renovation of that old instrument became to the people of Pilgrim a statement that the old culture of despair was replaced by one of life. The first sign of systemic disruption is anxiety.

At Pilgrim the very coming of Laurie caused anxiety among some longtime members. While they seemed to have little choice but to call the one person willing to come as their pastor, the decision nonetheless elevated anxiety because it disrupted the equilibrium. No matter that the equilibrium seemed to be leading to the congregation's death—the disequilibrium was still troubling. The organ became more than a sign that new things could happen. It was an emblem of a change in mentality from death to life. This new way included an invitation to those who differed to join in shaping new directions. Some did, some didn't. Laurie Hafner has practiced a combination of speaking her convictions and welcoming other points of view. If some don't support the decisions that are made, it is not because they haven't had the opportunity to air their differences. A healthy, open system will always make room for diverse perspectives, but it will not postpone decisions. Indecisiveness results in a system that is unable to respond to the demands placed on it by the world. Indecision will close a system.

The leaders of Lewinsville Presbyterian Church have discovered how complex a system's diversity can be. A congregational system can include historical traditions; current dynamics like values, decision-making processes, and communication; and various groups in the congregation. In particular the people at Lewinsville have learned that the interaction of group life and mission is essential for systemic health. Groups like to establish, preserve, and perpetuate themselves. The congregation's mission can push on the stability of groups, sometimes calling the groups to new tasks. This pressure can raise anxiety among those who want their groups to stay as they are. This call to mission can also lead to anxiety in the congregation as member groups are challenged to adapt to new responsibilities. Pastor Gary Pinder has a great capacity to live with this anxiety, but it has not always been simple for him to persuade lay leaders to be flexible. Most are willing these days, in part because of their great trust for Pinder, and because some of them feel welcome to bring to the congregation's work their gifts and skills. The tension between groups in the congregation and the congregation's missional direction remains challenging. But the effort to live with this tension offers people of varying opinions a way to enter the discussion. In other words, this struggle is taking place in full view of the congregation, and all who might otherwise resist it are encouraged to join the process.

Putting It Together

I found five pre-existing conditions or practices in the eight congregations I examined. It would not have been surprising to find some of these in a few of the congregations and other practices in the others. What is most significant is that all eight had developed all five of the conditions. They are not practices that arise without effort on the part of leaders. I heard stories about how these conditions developed. In each case the pastor's role was significant, both in articulating the importance of developing these conditions and in outright teaching and personal coaching of leaders to share in their development. We go now to responses to resistance that have less to do with the organization and more with the leaders' own capacities.

Individual Responses to Resistance

I found that leaders, particularly pastors, when faced with resistance, rely primarily on three responses, despite pre-existing conditions: (1) strong empathy and a resulting willingness to listen, (2) the courage to persist and act on conviction, and (3) a strong desire to teach. Not all eight of the pastors practice each of these modes of response. I will cite some congregations that were among those where each of these responses was used.

Empathic listening. The pastors and many lay leaders were caring practitioners of pastoral care. In all of the congregations people with diverse points of view were encouraged to give voice as decisions were being made. At points where real disruption occurred, particularly where resistance was at levels 5 through 7, and decisions had been made that were now being actively opposed, the capacity to listen was less common. Rabbi Edwin Friedman speaks of the importance of the pastor's being a "nonanxious presence." In the congregation, says church consultant Peter Steinke, "If leaders are as anxious and reacting as the people they serve, those served will not be served well."[5] It is the capacity of pastors and leaders to respond in a nonanxious way that serves them well when faced with resistance, particularly at higher levels. Tony Stanley and Gary Straub were especially strong in this capacity.

Stanley, with an ear for the long-standing members of the congregation, used his heart and skills for listening to offer a welcome response to the resistance that came when Peoples Congregational United Church of Christ began to change. Among those who had been there for many years and had given much to this congregation's life were some who simply did not appreciate this change in outreach and hospitality. While Tony and some lay leaders knew that the congregation's future depended on younger people becoming involved, this realization was not the primary reason for reaching out to them. Leaders of Peoples Church felt that the congregation was called to reach out to new people in the community. While Tony was committed to what Peoples was doing, his capacity to listen with love became a vital resource as he moved from parishioner to parishioner, inviting them to raise concerns. This was not only an important response in those years; it has stood time's test and remains one of the primary assets Tony brings to ministry at Peoples Congregational Church.

At First Christian Church, Frankfort, Gary Straub responds to resistance with "Let's talk, let's pray together, and let's talk some more." The changes that have come to this congregation have not been sudden. The outcomes sought—laypeople coming to know their spiritual gifts and being empowered to use them in ministry; a team approach to the life of the congregation—are best reached by an evolutionary, not a revolutionary process. These outcomes do not come in sudden bursts, but require patient teaching, prayer, and planning. In time, though, as these changes moved beyond adjustments and retoolings to transformation, those who had other opinions resisted. Despite the opportunities for dialogue and participation offered, some still questioned. Because they perceived the extent of changes, their resistance rose to levels 6 and 7. Gary's empathy, a willingness to know resisters' feelings without being compelled to agree with their points of view, was a vital pastoral tool. He used it and served as a model for lay leaders.

Courage to act on convictions. Courage, the strength to face danger, is a quality that some have and others do not. A simple faith-based understanding of courage was stated by the evangelist Billy Graham: "We can rest assured that God will give us strength when we have none of our own."[6] All of the pastors in the churches I studied are people of courage. Even people who resist strongly can be struck by the determination of a leader to stand firmly for his or her convictions. The pastors I observed did not take a "firm stand" in a way that would run over those who disagreed with what was happening. A unique brand of faithful courage comes to some who take a stand while affirming the right of every person to walk a different path. Delores Carpenter and John Peterson were said by lay leaders to have responded with this kind of courage.

Delores's tenure at Michigan Park Christian Church had been marked by significant changes. Not all of these were changes that she had named and called for, but she has practiced a style of ministry that opens doors for faithful transitions. One of the most difficult areas, as related in the case study, has been governance. The congregation had a history, from its denominational roots and its own choices, of making certain tasks and decisions strictly the business of laity, and the pastor did not need to be involved. One such area was property matters. Delores found that certain people had a virtual stranglehold on property matters, not allowing other lay leaders, much less the pastor, even to comment on decisions and actions. In time this power center opened up, and now on a daily basis the pastor is a partner in decision-making about property matters. Before this change, however, Delores found herself under fire—often accused of trying to gain unnecessary power. Lay leaders state that her capacity to remain calm under this kind of stress is an outgrowth of her faith-based courage. One of the direct results of her grace under pressure for the whole life of the congregation has been an increase in lay leaders' capacity to be nonanxious and persistent in their ministry.

John Peterson has had many opportunities to step out in faithful courage. Perhaps most notable was his decision to withdraw from the ministers' fellowship when the group condemned the decision of Alfred Street Baptist Church to ordain a woman as a deacon. The separation set him, formally at least, apart from colleagues and an important support system. He risked his career. John tells a story of his childhood on a farm. When he rode bareback on his family's horse, Morgan, he would always have to dismount and lead the horse through all the cow gates, because the horse was trained to stop for them. John says he learned then that sometimes you have to "get off the horse and lead it. You just have to be out front." Lay leaders speak far more openly than John does about this quality in him, even calling it a "good kind" of stubbornness. It isn't the kind of characteristic that people are trained to practice. John says that it is given by God.

A strong desire to teach. Some pastors are gifted communicators, both because they have great skills and they love to use them. It is particularly striking to see people who communicate well in the midst of crisis. A quality of great value in responding to resistance at any level is the capacity to reach out with information—less to try to change minds than to be clear about the initiative at which the resistance is directed. The speaker cannot insist that the audience agree with the information or respond to it in any particular way. The leader simply needs to interpret and explain, without defensiveness, so people will know what is happening. This practice may not change minds, but it will enable people who disagree to make clear decisions about whether to support an effort.

At Geist Christian Church Randy Spleth uses information and his ability to impart it in effective ways. Within the past year the judicatory of which his congregation is part asked every congregation to engage in a study about the ordination of gay men and lesbians. Randy and the congregation's leaders decided that the Geist congregation needed to decide whether to engage in the study. Voices were heard speaking both for and against the study. In a series of congregational events Spleth shared an overview of information from the Bible about both the subject of the proposed study and the question of when dialogue is appropriate and important. He gave this presentation without saying whether he believed that they should participate. People were invited to voice their concerns, pro and con, about participation. Finally the congregation made a decision about its involvement. The importance of informing members about issues has been stressed often at Geist. Randy's leadership over the years has included teaching about issues and decisions the congregation faces. Often this approach is used in response to resistance at all levels.

Gary Pinder and the lay leaders of Lewinsville Presbyterian Church often teach and encourage members about the congregation's goals and directions. It is not the pastor's intent to tell others what to think. Rather he wants to encourage others to consider some issues in new ways. This teaching has been particularly important at Lewinsville as long-established patterns of action are replaced by new approaches. Questions have been raised about developing mutual ministry among the laity and moving to a more focused sense of mission—raised largely by those who shaped and sustained prior approaches. It has been a special concern of Gary and the lay leaders that these dissenters not feel as though their work has been in vain. To this end, leaders have attempted to interpret the new directions, to show that these efforts are not competing with but building on the former approaches. Most of the resistance encountered to date has been in the 4-to-6 range. As the implications of these changes sink in and they are seen as truly transformative, resistance may rise to a higher level. By teaching about the changes, Gary and other leaders hope to engage resisters in an ongoing constructive dialogue about the congregation's life.

Some Lessons Learned

Among the impressive qualities of these eight pastors and the lay leaders who have learned to work with them is a combination of dissatisfaction with the status quo and a dedication to pastoral care and patience with the people they serve. Leadership teacher Jay Conger says, "Charismatic leaders are by vocation change agents. They see the shortcomings of any situation." He quotes Arch McGill, former head of AT&T: "I have an intolerance for 'what is' and 'what has been.' I believe everything can be done better."[7]

While this sense of situations being incomplete is alive in these pastors, the desire to care for all, including those who resist the most, is important to them. The grace to practice both of these gifts of God's spirit—of restlessness with things as they are and care for all people—is perhaps what marks well the leader who is able to respond with grace to resistance in the congregation's life. For while change continues to happen, not all people like change, and not all pastors lead it well. Leading change requires a receptive hearing for those who question it. This combination of graces appears to be the most significant quality of these eight extraordinary pastors and the leaders they coach day in and day out. It is my hope that pastors and lay leaders can learn the skill of listening for and hearing resistance, for this ability will support them well as they seek to lead change in the congregation.

FOR REFLECTION

1. Think about the life cycle described in this chapter: formation, expansion, stabilization, breakdown, crisis. Where do you believe your congregation stands in this cycle?

2. Choose two congregations from the case studies presented (see chapter 3). What are some signs of those congregations' work in developing the pre-existing conditions?

3. Can you identify additional qualities of congregational leaders that help them respond effectively to resistance?

Chapter 5

Leaders and Power

The message came by e-mail.

Dear Bishop:
You will want to know that Rev. Harrison was told by the mod-
erator last evening at executive council that when the congre-
gation meets on Sunday there will be a motion made to dismiss
him as pastor of St. John's Church.

A friend

No matter the circumstances leading to this note; no matter, even, the absence of a signature, the question must be asked: Is this a proper or improper use of power on the part of the moderator?

Does power matter in the congregation's life? Do leaders of congregations have power? If so, how much power and what kind? What purpose does power serve in the congregation? Honestly, is power a bad thing? Is it ethical to use? Can deep differences like these between the moderator and the pastor cited above be faced in healthy ways or must such differences mean a power struggle that could sap much of the congregation's energy?

Most important for our purposes, what is the role of power in leadership initiatives and resistance to them?

The capacity to initiate change in the congregation, and to respond to resistance to change; indeed, even the energy to resist changes—all require power.

A DEFINITION OF POWER

I want to propose a working definition of power for leaders in congregations: *Power is the ability and willingness to mobilize and use God-
given skills, gifts, and other resources in ethically appropriate ways to
achieve a desired outcome that will benefit the congregation.*

This is, to be sure, an idealistic definition of power. But we must see
what can be to set goals about what we will aspire to be. When power is
exercised as defined, underlying assumptions prescribe its use:

1. Those using power in this way are willing to be accountable to God and
   to the church.
2. This power ought to be used within a clear ethical framework, and it
   begins with love and respect for all of God's children.
3. Power should not be used in ways that manipulate people; fairness and
   choice will guide its use.
4. Leaders are responsible for discerning the best ways to use power.
5. Those who use power must be mindful of its effects on all parts of the
   congregation.
6. The whole congregation will not always agree with a particular use of
   power.

Power and Faith

Power is named at least 100 times in scripture. Sometimes it is ascribed to
God. Often the word describes people trying to live in faithfulness to God.
An important instance is Jesus' statement as he prepares to leave his dis-
ciples:

> You shall receive power when the Holy Spirit has come upon you;
> and you shall be my witnesses in Jerusalem, in all Judea and Samaria,
> and to the ends of the earth.
>
> Acts 1:8

In the Christian tradition no commission is more important than this one.
Jesus promises power, through the presence of the Holy Spirit. Often in the
Bible "spirit" is translated from the Hebrew word *ruach*, or *ruah*, also

meaning "wind," or the Greek *pneuma*, which also means "breath." These words suggest a force that moves in those who receive it. Reading on in the book of Acts, we see the effects of this spirit-generated power on Jesus' disciples.

In the best sense, the spirit is the power to which the definition above refers. I say "in the best sense" because the effect of the Holy Spirit is at times narrowed by some to mean that it brings power only through certain "gifts of the spirit" (*charismata*) like healing or speaking in tongues. Paul also says that leadership is an important gift of the Spirit (Rom. 12:8). Where leadership exercises power in the way defined earlier in this chapter, that power can be seen as the Holy Spirit moving.

Other Understandings of Power

It is important to compare our definition with other understandings of power. The interface of power and authority is an important element in understanding the work of leaders, says Ronald Heifetz, of the Kennedy School of Government at Harvard University. Authority "can be divided into two forms: formal and informal. With formal authority come the various powers of the office, and with informal authority comes the power to influence attitude and behavior beyond compliance."[1] Formal authority comes of *explicit* expectations one promises to meet. Informal authority comes from promising to meet implicit expectations, such as "trustworthiness, ability and civility."[2] In this understanding power *carries with it the authority to get certain things done.*

Another understanding of power, from Dudley Weeks, a teacher of conflict-resolution skills at American University, is "the capacity to act effectively and the ability to influence."[3] Weeks says, however, that "many people behave as though they see power as the ability to make others behave as they want them to."[4] When this happens, damaging conflicts can result because power is taken by one person who, in effect, coerces others into dependency. Weeks goes further as he explores steps toward conflict resolution, later defining power as "consisting of the attitudes, perceptions, beliefs, and behaviors that give people and groups the ability to act or perform effectively."[5]

All of these understandings of power offer the notion that power is about getting things done. Whether people use power ethically, not taking advantage of others, and acting only with their consent, or use it at their own whim, those with power get things done.

All of these definitions agree that power, in and of itself, is not value laden. It simply *is*. What is *done with it* attaches values to power. Power can corrupt, unless the one with power holds himself or herself accountable to others. If the powerful one refuses to be accountable, then that power will be used corruptly.

Power and Dependence

One of the critical aspects of using power in the faith community is its relationship to dependence. That is, do people use power to create dependence? If so, can this intention result in abuse of power? At what point does this happen?

Some suggest that it is in the nature of some human beings to be dependent. Years ago in a pastorate I had been working with a particular lay leadership group in an effort to clarify its role in the congregation. Group members had had an important responsibility in the past, but their duties had become quite unclear and their role weakened. After a particularly hard-working session one member, Chuck, came up to me and, mustering all his military knowledge, said, "Chris, you know best. If you'll just tell us what to do, we'll do it." What an opportunity! I cannot say that there haven't been times when I've dreamed of church members saying this to me, or, more recently in a judicatory office, times when I would have liked whole congregations to say it. I had to constrain myself, though, and say simply, "That's not the way to do it, Chuck. We can't move on my say-so alone. It will get us nowhere. This is a process and decision that we need to share." He was puzzled. I certainly hope that in time he understood that the kind of dependency he suggested would fail to accomplish the task of enabling the group to clarify and undertake its role.

It isn't uncommon for clergy and even some lay leaders to struggle with dependency issues. It has been suggested that one motivation for people entering the ordained ministry is the prospect of having others depend on them. Some people might, consciously or unconsciously, even manipulate a situation to cultivate dependency. Consciously creating dependence is an abuse of power.

Underlying the use of power in a congregation's life must be a continuing passion to empower others. This motive stands in sharp contrast to the power used to cultivate the dependence of others. Examples from Bible stories illustrate empowerment. Beginning with God's promise to Abram and Sarai (Gen. 12:4-5) through kings, queens, prophets, and Jesus and the apostles, these narratives are loaded with such acts as anointing, laying hands of blessing on others, and using sacraments and prayers to empower others. The premise of power as an agent in a congregation's life is that power is used so that leaders may impart to others the power that God intends for them.

THE CONGREGATION AND POWER

Power is the ability and willingness to mobilize and use God-given skills, gifts and other resources in ethically appropriate ways to achieve a desired outcome that will benefit the congregation.

This definition is certainly not the only approach to power in congregations. Indeed, this one might be called a definition of "good power." Power in its most basic form can be described as "the ability to do or act."[6] We could argue that power in and of itself is neutral, and that it is how power is used that matters.

If the definition above applies to "good power," how can we describe "bad power?" When power is exercised to impose values that hurt and diminish others or when power is used simply to get the user's way with no concern for others' opinions, it is "bad power."

One's power can be increased by a variety of factors. Sometimes those who give large amounts of money use this generosity as influence to get their way. In some congregations power can derive from the supposed wisdom of seniority. I recall a conversation with a wealthy member of the Spring Lake Church, who had often gotten his way because of his giving, and who thought seniority should carry power. He had lost a difficult struggle over a congregational membership policy. The "winning opposition," as he put it, was led by a young man, relatively new to the congregation, but persuasive and smart. The old gentleman said to me, "You know, he's only been a member here for five years. Doesn't it seem unfair that he won?" How could I answer my friend with whom I so disagreed?

Power can also take the form of the capacity to give rewards of position and prestige, appealing to those who have need for recognition or security. Unlike organizations whose participants receive pay for their services, the church offers different rewards. They are less tangible and visible and thus, like money, can be used in devious ways. At times even theological or spiritual authority can be used to intimidate or reward people, as such benefits as eternal life are assured those who follow properly. It may seem unbelievable that this could happen, but history reminds us that the Protestant Reformation grew in part out of a strong sense on the part of leaders like Martin Luther that the power of promising eternal rewards was being abused by church leaders.

Power can also be used by commanding attention, communicating effectively, and resisting initiatives in a congregation. All of these can reflect either appropriate or inappropriate uses of power.

Power and Trust

Trust is the quality that makes "good power" work. Jack Harris said, "The personal authenticity of the minister, priest or rabbi is the greatest strength of any congregation. The inauthenticity of the clergy is the greatest weakness of organized religion."[7] I think of trustworthiness as an aspect of authenticity, and I agree with Harris to a point, that being that a congregation's strength is also related to the authenticity of lay leadership. Many congregations have survived a pastor who lost their trust because they had lay leaders who were trustable. Clergy and lay leaders are not always trusted equally.

Jack Gibb, a social psychologist who studied trust development in hundreds of groups, says that trust "implies instinctive, unquestioning belief in and reliance upon something."[8] While for many the word "instinctive" may not be accurate, still the reality of "belief in and reliance upon" is vital to trust. Different leaders can elicit varied responses, and pastors are not the only ones who can be trusted.

Congregations will grant authority to people in certain roles. Under most circumstances the pastor is given a certain amount of authority because she holds that position. Lay leader roles are accorded authority as well. With authority comes a degree of power to do particular things. This is *formal authority* as Heifetz describes it. *Informal authority*, however, runs deeper, with the expectations of that authority being implicit rather than explicit. Formal authority comes from *explicit* expectations a person promises to meet. Informal authority comes from promising to meet *implicit* expectations, such as "trustworthiness, ability and civility."[9]

Linking trust to his understanding of charismatic leadership, organizational behaviorist Jay Conger says, "The charismatic leader builds exceptional trust through personal risk-taking, unconventional expertise, and *self-sacrifice* [italics added]. . . . They accomplish this by showing concern for followers' needs rather than for their own self-interest."[10] Here is another list of power sources. I am reminded of Laurie Hafner's reflections about how genuine pastoral care has earned her the credibility to lead in some new ways at Pilgrim Congregational, though she didn't love people just so she could get her way. Deep love can't be turned off and on like water from a faucet.

We can say, then, that in the congregation a degree of authority and the consequent power are given to those who hold certain offices—pastor, moderator, vestry member, elder, etc.—and power can grow as trust grows. Trust deepens when people come to know that they can place themselves in this person's hands and they won't be abused there. Rather they will be supported, loved, and helped to grow.

I'll look more deeply at power and resistance at a later point, but it is important to say here that constructive resistance to leadership initiatives is more likely to be offered, and welcomed, when this kind of trust underlies relationships.

Sharing Leadership

A characteristic of power as we define it here is that under most circumstances, power is more naturally shared in a congregation. Yet even in a congregation where we might expect power to be shared, it can be exercised for personal gain rather than for *an outcome that will benefit the congregation.* The reason for sharing leadership is not that a collective wielding of power will mean more votes. Rather, sharing leadership is one way that pastors and lay leaders can demonstrate the mutual trust that is the very foundation of "good power."

A changing organization needs, as it changes, to be a prototype, or model, of the desired outcome of the change process. If we want to become a congregation where everyone feels included and welcomed, then the steps we take to get there must seek to include and welcome everyone. We need to *be* that congregation even as we *become* it. Thus, as Peoples

Congregational moved to become open to people of all generations and educational levels, Tony Stanley became a pastor to everyone, including those who felt excluded from this new emphasis. He worked hard at this task. As he put it, "They spoke, I listened." According to lay leaders, it has remained that way for 33 years.

Therefore a congregational leader, such as the pastor, can hardly invite and encourage people's trust (or assume it will be forthcoming) if he or she is unwilling first to trust other leaders. The words "trust me" ring hollow unless I trust you as well. It is the capacity, for example, to hold the vision alone and then to begin sharing it, and finally, even to cede the leadership to others, that marks the wisest power-filled leaders in the congregation.

The case studies discussed in chapters 3 and 4 show pastors who have been in these ministries for at least 10 years. As long pastorates near their end, a true test of the depth of trust can be seen in the openness of the pastor to trust others, including, in most cases, an unknown successor, to lead on in this congregation's journey. This is trustworthiness, and herein is one of the basic sources of good power. I am struck, for example, by Gary Pinder's passion to participate in leading Lewinsville Presbyterian Church, as Phil stated it, to a point at which there will be "a cohesion that is not dependent on the presence and personality of a pastor." I believe that one of the visions of a pastor should be to make his or her job unnecessary.

Other persuasive arguments can be marshaled for sharing power. Sharing power gives the group access to its collective wisdom, creates opportunities for mutual support, and forms a broader pool of gifts, skills, and voices that can be used to involve more people. As members of a leadership team develop mutual trust and begin to trust the congregation, trust is given them in return. With this trust comes power to make decisions and to act in the interest of the congregation. Another assumption underlying the definition is that those with power are willing to be accountable, together, for their decisions and actions.

An important question lurks behind this discussion: Can someone be phony and exercise power in the congregation? We have to answer that in some cases one can, for a time. It was in a large congregation that had been engaged in a brewing and divisive conflict where I heard several lay leaders say of their pastor, "He just doesn't like us. He will say one thing and do another, always blaming one of us when things go wrong. For a while we went along, believing him. Some still believe it. But now we know: he just doesn't like us." It was in his unwillingness to accept responsibility for his own mistakes that the leaders found their pastor unable to trust enough to share power with them. Yes, a phony can last for a while. Tragically, whether that person is a pastor or a lay leader, it is not easy to extricate the congregation from the mess created by broken trust.

For this and many other reasons it is important, from the very beginning of a pastorate or the induction of new lay leaders, to deliberately develop trust among a congregation's leaders. Time spent in team-building, sharing hopes for the work they hope to do together, clarifying roles and mutual expectations, and praying together, can serve them well in beginning to build mutual trust. Here also is a place where external resources such as the middle judicatory can be well used, as steps are taken early to provide the kind of foundation that will endure in good and tough times.

Ethics and Power in the Congregation

"Good power" might also be called "anticoercive power," indicating that the use of this form of power fails not only if it manipulates others, but also if it falls short of empowering and encouraging others to be engaged in the congregation's life. Those with power do not operate only in their own interest.

The ethical framework for the way anticoercive power is used is expressed in the philosopher Immanuel Kant's *categorical imperative*, that "each person will live in such fashion that the principles on which he [or she] acts can become those on which all should act."[11] This 18th-century ethical norm presses for responsible, accountable, community-focused actions.

To this end, then, those who use anticoercive power in the congregation recognize the worth of all people. They function not to bring others to their users' points of view, but to enhance the community of the faithful where each person can grow and experience the blooming of the gifts God has placed within.

It sounds like a naïve list of all the behaviors of good boys and girls, but honesty, mutual care, fairness, and decency will be the features of this power in action. The reason is important: unless power is used with fairness and respect, the final result of its use will be an unfair and unethical community. Some of the lay leaders at Michigan Park Church asked a question about their pastor, Delores Carpenter. As one said, "At one time people would do things to her and she wouldn't say anything. How can she be so loving? She sets an example." They gave part of the answer to their own question. "She sets an example." But the deeper answer is that she felt she had no choice. To be certain, she did have a choice. She could have struck back. But for what gain?

Faithful leaders know that the ethics of bad power reverberate in many ways. Such leadership can hurt others, sometimes permanently. It can damage the very goals leaders seek to achieve if they do not act in ways congruent with those lofty outcomes. Unethical leaders risk setting a bad example when they model behavior that is less than fair and just.

Change, Resistance, and Power

Both congregational change and resistance to change require power to make them happen. As we look at them, though, it is important to recognize that either can happen with the use of either coercive or anticoercive power. People in the church, as has been said, can be bullied and manipulated with money, promises of position, and even assurances of eternal life. People responding to initiatives can threaten to withhold participation or to cause outright disruption of congregational life.

My interest is in power activity that is anticoercive rather than coercive. We might even move to countercoercive power, power that not only opposes coercion, but that supports the very opposite, working for just and fair relations with people even as it seeks the desired outcome.

As the use of power becomes less coercive, fairer, and more just, the level of trust that makes "good power" will increase. This statement doesn't suggest that disagreements and resistance will cease to happen. It does mean that the congregation's capacity to manage them wisely with constructive dialogue and with hope for good outcomes will increase.

Figure 9
Scale of power use and resistance

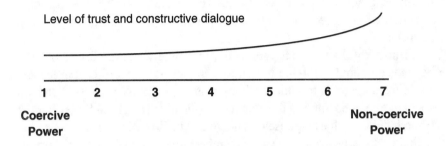

Level of trust and constructive dialogue

| 1 | 2 | 3 | 4 | 5 | 6 | 7 |

Coercive   Non-coercive
Power   Power

Figure 9 illustrates the reality that as the use of power becomes increasingly noncoercive, the trust required for constructive dialogue, including dialogue with those resisting an initiative, will increase. The interaction that follows is more likely to be open and respectful and to hold the promise of a good resolution, whether this means compromise or just more understanding among folk. As we explore power and change next, we will see the importance of noncoercive power.

Power and Change

The fairness with which power is used by leaders can strongly affect the willingness of members to endorse and support the changes the leaders initiate.

"He is very authoritarian. He likes to get his way. If the truth were told, I believe he'd rather my wife and I leave the church, because in some way we represent, to him at least, a hard-to-handle community of rational opposition to some of his ideas and actions."

This comment, made to me long ago, referred to the pastor of a midsized congregation that had undertaken changes that sparked some disputes. The lay leader who spoke was an active and committed steward. He seemed to me the kind of layperson whom you want on your side or who you assume is on the pastor's side. I was surprised at his strong words about a pastor who seemed to be well liked.

Power can be accumulated in many ways to make changes in the life of a congregation. No one who spends time in and around congregations for very long dares assume that all changes are brought about by people using purely anticoercive power. The power gained through knowledge of parishioners and some of their problems can be used coercively, as can the authority to grant status and recognition. Even the ability to give personal attention can be used abusively if the person seeks political support as a payback.

But faithful and creative ministry, in a time when the future of faith depends on people growing to maturity in their faith, requires that leaders move from coercive to anticoercive forms of power. When John Peterson encountered opposition to the plan to raze the historic Alfred Street Baptist Church building, his response was not to call in the bulldozers but to lead in seeking alternatives. Patience gave members time to find community groups interested in helping preserve this history while allowing the congregation to build a larger and more functional building.

Whatever the degree of change, from level 1 (maintaining) to level 7 (transforming), the use of anticoercive power is important. It is crucial to note that coercive methods can often appear innocent, even seeming to be absentmindedness. A leader who fails to hear someone's comment, carelessly forgets a particular vote, does not pay attention to the quorum in a meeting, or even repeats a favorite idea one more time without allowing the skeptics to raise their questions, may seem harmless, but can appear very manipulative to members. It isn't just overt and intentional coercive steps that can have a destructive effect on an organization's process.

It is unfortunately true that great vision is not always presented in the best of fashions. The argument here is not to curb dreams and goals for change but to learn ways to share these and listen to responses so that those within the whole congregational community will feel that they matter. Great will be the rewards (in congregational support, solid and fair discussions of issues and ideas, people with new gifts and talent stepping forward, and even sleep-filled nights) for those leaders who practice the outcomes they aspire to for their congregations. The product is important. Of this there can be no doubt. But the product can end up in shipwreck if the voyage isn't piloted wisely. The leaders' wielding of power, whether coercive or noncoercive, will affect the degree to which change will gain support in the congregation.

Power and Resistance

Leaders who use power in a noncoercive way will invite honest and hearty resistance. People will not resist their methods but the initiatives being proposed. Some would argue that it's better to push changes right on through than to give those who resist the time to speak. Illustrating this kind of leadership is an old story from the political world about the fabled Sam Rayburn, longtime speaker of the U.S. House of Representatives, who presided at quadrennial presidential nominating conventions of the Democratic Party. If a desired motion was made, "Mr. Sam" would say, "All in favor, say 'Aye.' All opposed say 'Aye'; the Ayes have it and the motion passes." Resistance wasn't given a chance.

Sometimes religious rules, like canon law in some Christian traditions, give formal authority and the resulting power to people in certain offices. Wise leaders will use this formal authority in anticoercive ways. Where a question is open, I believe it is possible and in the best interest of congregations to work consciously toward anticoercive approaches to decisions. This means that fair and honest resistance will be welcomed and that leaders will see in heartfelt resistance the opportunities for dialogue that may bring a better result than the one first proposed. Recognizing that there is always more than one way to do something, this kind of openness will offer opportunities for leaders to gain insights to which they may have previously been blind.

A model of feedback in use for many years, called "Johari's Window," can help us understand our blind spots:

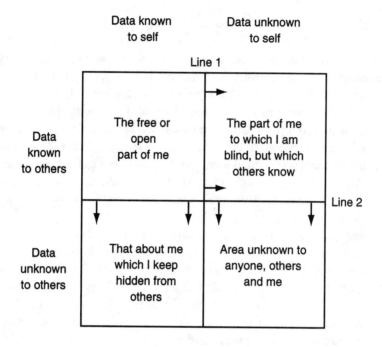

Figure 10
Johari's Window

Named for its creators, Joe Luft and Harry Ingraham, this "window" tells us what information is available to us.[12] While the model is used primarily for an individual's self-awareness, it contains truth for organizations as well. The "window panes" that are particularly important in organizational life are those on the right side. Significant feedback, openness to dialogue, and a willingness to listen to resistance can move line 1 to the right, indicating that less data is unavailable to the congregation. The mystery of such a rich exchange is that in the process this dialogue can lead to common insights new to all, revelation, and line 2 will move downward as well. We learn more about our plans and hopes and our life together as a congregation. The area known to others and to ourselves is enlarged.

I said in chapter 2 that *resistance happens when the need for stability and the changing mission of a congregation push so hard on one another that resolution of the two becomes elusive and has to be intentionally sought after.* It does not follow that resolution will or even should happen every time there is resistance. If it does come, it will be only after much negotiation and compromise.

It is more likely that a pastoral solution can come of a good dialogue, and even though those resisting may come to the conclusion that they will not get their way, the fact that they have been heard is important. Miss Carrie used to say to her pastor, "You know, what I like about you is that you always listen to me when I disagree with something that is going on here. You seldom do what I suggest, but you listen and that means a lot to me in these changing times. Most young folks like you just don't listen to old fogies like me."

Had she never said a word to the pastor, meaning that she never took issue openly with an action in the church, it would have signaled either that little was happening or that resistance was suppressed. The danger is that church leaders often confuse the absence of negative feedback with good health and happiness. From the beginning it has been the premise of this study that resistance can be a sign of vitality.

This is not to idealize resistance. Resistance can be whiny, messy grumpiness. It can be the action of a person or persons who are forever seeking power in a congregation and just won't go along with the majority. But lest this view of resistance prevail, we need to remember that it can also be an authentic expression of concern that things are moving too fast, too slow, too much, or too little, or simply that this process could be helped if something else were done.

Anticoercive uses of power welcome differences of opinion. Existing resistance invites more resistance. It announces the fact that whatever happens is happening in the open, and if there are differences, we can bring them up and give them fair attention. The congregation that uses power anticoercively celebrates the open resistance that takes place because it can mean two things: what is taking place is meaningful enough to elicit resistance, and the place allows, indeed welcomes the airing of differences without the condemnation of anyone.

The Anatomy of Change

Leadership initiatives and resistance both produce change. The one brings change from what is; the other would change the climate of decision making, sometimes leading the congregation to revert to former ways.

Leaders are helped if they approach change with purpose and under-standing.

I have found that two core principles of change, developed and de-scribed by Ronald Heifetz in the book *Leadership Without Easy Answers*, are helpful tools for leaders. Heifetz argues that first, we need to under-stand and distinguish between technical and adaptive problems,[13] and sec-ond, we need to know appropriate leadership processes for both, but par-ticularly for adaptive situations.[14]

In a "technical" situation the problem is definable, and its solution is clear. That is, the resolution of the problem requires technical work. Heifetz uses the doctor-patient relationship to illustrate this concept. It is one in which "the patient's expectations are realistic and the problem can be de-fined and treated."[15] The problem can be addressed, even fixed, by treating the illness. An infection is treated with antibiotics, a broken bone is stabi-lized and kept in place until healing occurs, or a wound is stitched so that new growth can knit skin and tissue together again. Here, definable prob-lems and definable solutions add up to success.

In "adaptive" situations, on the other hand, the problem and the solution are not definable and technical resolution cannot be found. "The situation calls for leadership that induces learning. . . . Learning is required both to define problems and implement solutions."[16] Adaptive situations call for change and understanding of new methods of living, fresh ways of being community. Heifetz offers the example of a physician's care for a cancer patient (who appears to be terminally ill) and his family. The work done in this relationship shows that even when a solution is not obvious or possible, the situation can be managed with wisdom and care so that the participants come to accept and cope with what they are facing.

In religious settings people often yearn for solutions. In personal faith matters, such factors as guilt and illness can bring hunger for an answer that will resolve matters as quickly as possible. Likewise, in a congregation's life together, it is normal to wish for quickly managed solutions to all sorts of problems. Some problems can be solved quickly, for they are technical. But matters of change, like other concerns that are part of the congregation's life as a system, do not always lend themselves to simple fixes. It is some-times tempting to offer technical answers to adaptive challenges, but to do so can create serious problems, as the challenges continue and the people are disappointed that the answer "didn't work." Such inadequate answers will often lead to congregational decline. The allure, for example, of promising rewards like numerical growth and even material prosperity in exchange for certain behaviors in a congregation faced with problems, is an abuse of the power of leadership. It is coercive.

Among the congregations I studied it was clear that in churches and pastorates with long histories, adaptive change was more common when major transitions took place. In congregations with shorter stories, or where revitalization depended on rapid actions, technical solutions were more often turned to. Though this difference doesn't always hold, I was struck by its frequency.

At Lewinsville Presbyterian Church, where Gary Pinder has served as pastor for 33 years, the process of discerning and moving toward a new identity is one that has no clear and definable goal. Rather it is a process of "moving toward" a different way of being the church. First Christian, Frankfort, has likewise been engaged in a new way of calling out the gifts of the laity. This process has been received in a mixed way, with resisters questioning the way this approach to gifts challenges what seemed to them a perfectly good way of using the skills of the laity. If members have learned nothing else, they have discovered that such a change takes years.

In contrast, at Largo Community Church, founded in the early 1970s and still led by Pastor Jack Morris, most major decisions can be spelled out and seen clearly as pro-or-con issues. Likewise, Pilgrim Congregational in Cleveland made its first major decision, the restoration of the old organ, in a short time, and it seemed, in retrospect, to be a "no-brainer," an obvious technical solution.

The resistance brought to these different kinds of decisions also differs. Certainly technical decisions can produce more open and obvious resistance, with alternatives presented to the solutions proposed. When the resistance relates to an adaptive process, it appears that those resisting have to hunker down and plan to outlast the process if the resistance is going to affect and change what is happening.

This difference is certainly worth noting as we seek to understand the nature of decisions that face congregations and the resistance that may appear in response to these decisions.

It Is Never Simple, Is It?

Any time that change and resistance are dealt with in the congregation, we are working with a complex reality. The congregation is still a social system, made up of interacting parts. When one part is changed, all will be touched. If a part over here has a problem, parts over there will feel the effects.

Some years ago, while serving a congregation, I made an effort to evaluate the ways in which one decision, to lease space to a community organization for a Head Start center, would touch various organizations and people in the congregation. I learned that no one in that congregation would be unaffected by the decision. Whether someone resisted the decision to lease, was fully supportive, or said he or she could not care less, everyone was affected. There would be added income to balance the budget, but rooms would be used that had heretofore been reserved for church school. We would incur added custodial costs, have to share a kitchen, and appease neighbors frightened by this new program. New people would come to worship. The list seemed endless. But isn't that the way it is in a social system, where all parts are related?

Power, whether used coercively or in a countercoercive fashion, will have effects that reach further that we anticipate. But power is always present. The question is, will it be used to bring about change or resist change? And will it be used to work in a way that is in the best interest of the congregation and its members?

FOR REFLECTION

1. Name some ways that *formal* power is used in your congregation.

2. Name some ways that *informal* power is used.

3. What gives power to leaders in your congregation?

4. Can you identify ways in which power has been *abused* in the church?

5. List examples of *coercive* and *anticoercive* uses of power.

6. Has resistance arisen in your congregation? Have those who resisted had the power to be heard? What gave them the power to be heard?

7. Cite examples of technical and adaptive change in your congregation.

CHAPTER 6

Integrating Resistance
into the Congregation's Life

It is my hope that congregations will value the benefits of resistance enough to invite, hear, and learn from resistance as part of the congregation's continuing life. This capacity requires a climate in which people feel free to voice their concerns.

Resistance is expressed in every congregation. But will that resistance be heard, much less given attention? Though it would be absurd to consider institutionalizing resistance (imagine a "Department of Resistance"!), a nonanxious willingness to hear the voices of resistance will benefit a congregation and deepen the congregation's character. In this final chapter I will do three things: define a positive initiative><resistance cycle, offer readers suggestions for doing initiative><resistance case studies of their own congregations, and finally, list some "rules for the road" for managing initiatives and resistance in congregational life.

A Constructive Initiative><Resistance Cycle

The ways to respond to resistance in the congregation are numerous. In informal conversations about this book I have become accustomed to raised eyebrows and puzzled expressions as friends familiar with congregational life respond to the very idea of such a study. Some have even asked: "Why would you want to study resistance? Isn't it just bad?" I then tell them that a congregation without resistance is an unhealthy place, either because it doesn't allow opposition to be expressed or because the absence of resistance is a sign of a dying—or dead—congregation. Moreover, failing to welcome resistance is at best to miss suggestions, fresh ideas, and a sense of the congregation's tolerance for change.

So we can resist resistance by ignoring it and hoping it will go away, by refusing to hear it, by letting people express it but then ignoring it, or by hearing it and responding nondefensively. If the reader is among those more likely to be on the resisting than the initiating side of things, please understand that your perspective is more likely to be heard if you offer it in the same spirit with which I encourage leaders to receive it—with fairness, trust, and the love of the church at heart.

The diagram below is an image of a cycle of initiative and resistance in the congregation. The two ovals begin to move apart at the point of the initiative/decision for change. Resistance begins to be expressed as differences in interest between those who initiate change and those who resist become clear. As the expression of resistance begins to take its own path, the inner oval separates from the outer oval, the path of the initiative for change. When leaders respond to the resistance by hearing it, seeking to name its sources, and understanding it, the oval paths remain in parallel, not yet moving closer together. As some resolution is reached, whether a decision to change the initiative through compromise or simply an agreement to disagree with respect and care for one another, the oval paths begin to move toward each other. Their convergence represents the shared commitment of both leaders and resisters to the faithful and healthy life of the congregation.

I am fully aware that this simple model is an ideal representation of the interaction of leaders and resisters, and of the dynamics of change and resistance. I am also certain that strong and faithful congregational leaders will, perhaps after raising their eyebrows, see the value of trying to integrate resistance into the congregation's life.

Figure 11

A constructive initiative><resistance cycle for the congregation

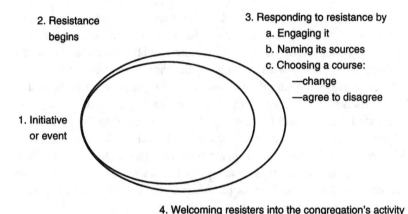

2. Resistance
begins

3. Responding to resistance by
a. Engaging it
b. Naming its sources
c. Choosing a course:
—change
—agree to disagree

1. Initiative
or event

4. Welcoming resisters into the congregation's activity

1. *The initiative or event that stimulates resistance.* An "event" refers to leadership initiatives, possible programs, a sermon or sermons, a policy decision, or any of many other interventions that may generate resistance. Congregational leaders are responsible and accountable for taking initiatives. But initiatives are not the only events that can stimulate resistance. Community demographic changes, unexpected disasters, leadership transitions, and unanticipated numbers of new members are among events that may elicit resistance. Each holds the potential for destabilizing the congregation.

2. *The resistance begins.* Resistance arises in response to events that destabilize or could potentially destabilize a congregation. To call it a "response," though, does not mean it always follows the event. While resistance is more likely to follow an initiative, those who resist may anticipate the initiatives, just as those who lead need to anticipate resistance. It is when leaders not only fail to anticipate resistance, but refuse to acknowledge and at least hear it, that problems crop up. Then the formula becomes

more like this: INITIATIVE>resistance, or even INITIATIVE>! (that is, "No resistance tolerated here"). On the other hand, when initiatives and resistance flow and people can teach each other about their points of views and the values they cherish, a healthy balance can be achieved in the system.

3. *Responding to resistance.* Congregational leaders can respond to resistance in a variety of ways. Often responses will be shaped by the degree of investment the leaders have in the intervention that generates the resistance. It is important for leaders to understand their own investment as they come face to face with resistance. Lacking this awareness, leaders may react in ways that aren't constructive. For example, Laurie Hafner and lay leaders at Pilgrim Congregational informally agreed that, as much as they cared that gay and lesbian people be welcomed in their congregation, they needed to hear and acknowledge expressions of resistance. They could have ignored it, refused to speak to the resisters, belittled resisters, or acted as though resistance was unacceptable. They chose instead to be just as inclusive of those resisting as they hoped the congregation would be welcoming of gay men and lesbians.

3a. *Engaging the resistance.* It is of utmost importance to know that hearing doesn't mean agreeing. Governments that are at odds, even competing with one another (for example, the United States and the former Soviet Union throughout the Cold War), continue to maintain diplomatic relations. At times the one who reaches out to hear resistance may fear that the very act of listening compromises his or her capacity to respond. Edwin Friedman, a pioneer in systems application to social organizations, tells us that, in organizational life, an "emotional triangle" is a way one can get "caught in the middle as the focus of an unresolved issue; "when any two parts of a system become uncomfortable with one another, they will 'triangle in' focus upon a third person . . . as a way of stabilizing their own relationship with one another."[1] Friedman goes on to say that "maintaining a non-anxious presence" is the key to lowering the anxiety of both parties. If one is "triangled," then that person, perhaps the one trying to "hear the resistance," becomes the most vulnerable" in the triangle.[2]

The point, of course, is to hear without feeling compelled to agree, giving personal support to resisters without taking their side. In the very act of hearing we show respect. Sometimes one who holds a different opinion will construe the very fact of having been heard as an act of agreement on the part of the hearer. It is important for the hearer to be quite clear. The purpose of hearing is to increase communication and therefore community. Resisters and hearers alike need to learn the value of this level of communication: it strengthens community without betraying the principles of either leader or resister.

Some religious organizations have particular people identified to hear and engage those whose point of view differs from that of the leadership. I said earlier that setting up something like a Department of Resistance would be absurd. However, there can be a place where people who "think otherwise" can go with concerns. Some congregations have "town meetings" from time to time just to give people a safe place to voice opinions. One congregation, as it sought to make a good decision about relocation, held a series of listening conferences and went out of the way to invite people to look critically at the idea of relocation. The information gained when resistance is heard can be invaluable.

To engage the resistance means to give attention, to recognize the views offered in the resistance. Sometimes resistance is expressed in less-than-obvious ways. At a time when First Church was undergoing changes in worship style, one lay leader took it as his responsibility to approach the pastor and music director regularly with a laundry list of problems about what was happening. The conversation would always begin with the line "Several people have told me that they don't like the hymn selections lately," or "They're saying that we need to start the prelude before the appointed worship hour." The pastor's reaction was always, "Ask the 'several people' to talk with me. Don't let them use you." In reality the pastor was missing the point. "Several people," it was safe to assume, always included this particular lay leader. A more appropriate response would have been to engage him in discussing the reasons for his concerns and why he chose this way to express them. Actually, I was the pastor in this situation. I look back on my response and ask myself what might have been gained had I reacted less defensively, and responded more transparently.

Transparency is a crucial value in congregational life. Hidden agendas don't wear well in healthy congregations. Indeed, because they breed mistrust, hidden agendas, like secret keeping, weaken systems.

To engage the voices of resistance may mean seeing people in a new light. Gifts heretofore hidden might emerge from resisters. Iris, a 40-something woman who had earlier been a loyal kitchen worker, began asking question after question about everything the congregation's spiritual and pastoral care team was doing. Some of her queries elicited information that showed that the team was not strong. Finally, despite some team members' irritation at her, she was asked to join the team just because she showed so much interest in this part of congregational life. She was a most gifted and spiritually open member of the team. People came to call on her, more than any other team member, for wisdom, pastoral care, and presence. All of this came about because she persisted in resisting, and someone heard her as more than an irritant.

3b. *Naming the sources of resistance.* Important in responding to resistance is being able to name the source, the sometimes fertile ground that gives growth to resistance. Seen through system eyes, this "naming" will point to pressures that might push back at the change to keep the system from becoming destabilized.

In the human body such sources might include too little sleep, too much exercise, a hormonal imbalance, a bipolar illness, significant work-related stress—the list is endless. We know that a system seeks balance or "homeostasis: the tendency of any set of relationships to strive perpetually, in self-corrective ways, to preserve the organizing principle of its existence."[3] Often, though, that balance is maintained to the point of rigidity, causing the system to become closed. Leadership initiatives will arise to challenge that rigidity because, as we have said, living systems change, or they die. Resisters respond to counter the change.

What was the source of the tension that led the resistance to rise? Was it fear of change, uneasiness with the change being proposed? Was it apprehension that a good, stable, and going enterprise would be disrupted, or concern that this good thing would soon be taken for granted? Was it irritation that certain contributions and opinions were being ignored, or a genuine desire to make contributions and offer opinions in the hope of helping the congregation?

It is easy enough to dismiss resistance as mere whininess. We do so at two costs, though. The first is the loss of whatever contribution might be missed in the overlooked resistance. The second is the loss of information about the system, the congregation's ongoing health and progress.

3c. *Choosing a course.* Early in my ministry, fight and flight were my options for responding to resistance. When people disagreed with me, I would either fight them with every ounce of brain I could muster, or I'd deny the very existence of their opposition. After about five years of pain and an additional five years of high-quality training and difficult self-assessment, I realized the dead-end alley I had walked into and the fresh paths that were available to be taken.

There are two possible next steps: change or an agreement to disagree. Either will fail without a climate of trust between leaders and resisters (see preconditions in chapter 4).

The first option is to change the initiative. If resistance is invited and welcomed, and change offered as an option, only for leaders to find out that despite the openness, there is no chance that change will come, then some will perceive that trust has been violated. There are degrees of change that can be applied to the initiative. The most obvious degree is to alter the basic idea or even develop a new idea. Compromise is a form of change in which the best is taken from each part, the initiative and the resistance. Mediation may be needed to arrive at the best compromise, but the outcome can be a solution at least somewhat satisfactory to all.

If it is clear that a way to change cannot be found after genuine efforts, an agreement to disagree should be sought. The important transformation is the understanding, by both initiators and resisters, that they and their opinions matter. Those who initiate change must be willing to listen to opinions and strategies far different from their own to show that they really do care about all the members. The truth must be that all people matter. All opinions matter. Not all opinions may be reflected in the final product, but all people must be treated with care and respect.

4. *Welcoming resisters into the congregation's activity.* Overt ways of welcoming resisters back into the life of the congregation should be employed. These may range from personal assurances of the importance of a resister's participation to more public events that cite that involvement. I have been told by many people in congregations that they are regarded as something like outsiders because they resist a lot. Some take pride in being so identified. It's not a pride that can last well for a lifetime. To be considered the "resident gadfly" can get old.

While it is important to make this a genuine welcome, it is just as important for resisters to reenter with sincerity. Nothing will diminish the importance of a resister's ideas faster than to find out that this person resists just to be resisting.

Ideally, in a healthy congregation the person who resists one idea should feel empowered to be an initiative leader the next time round.

An unproductive feature of some congregations is that certain people wear lifetime labels like "leader" and "resister." Because both roles are important, it is my hope that people who love their congregations will be ready to lead or resist as they believe themselves led.

To welcome resisters, then, is to celebrate both their willing participation in, and their importance to, the congregation's life. It is also a time to celebrate the open character of community the congregation seeks to exemplify.

5. *How can we implement this cycle?* I believe that putting the cycle into action is more a matter of attitude and the quality of the congregation's life than of any particular form. That is, rather than try to craft an organizational place for the welcoming of resistance, the congregation would do best to work at the pre-existing conditions described in chapter 4. The cycle will be useless without those conditions: a context of mutual trust, shared leadership, vision and teaching of the vision, spiritual formation, and tolerance for change.

Leadership for the cycle ideally should come from established congregational leaders rather than from members specially designated for the task, unless with that designation comes a congregational affirmation of the role. The pastor and lay leaders will do well to immerse themselves in the cycle and its possibilities for their congregation's life. The whole congregation also needs to examine the cycle from time to time to see if it is being followed. This cycle can be of particular value if all members have the opportunity to see its possibilities. Some may fear that following this cycle will only invite resistance. They may be right. But the resistance invited will likely be helpful—not the kind that gets under the skin of leaders because it nags rather than contributes to the congregation's life and health.

A Living Case Study

I hope you will see the value of the tools offered next and use them to your congregation's advantage. You are invited, even encouraged, to use the suggestions and questions that will follow to conduct a case study of your own congregation.

The purpose of this case study is to enable you and a team of fellow congregation members to get a picture of the health of your congregation as to its willingness to welcome resistance. Is it a place open to hearing and working with resistance for the good of the congregation?

The following format for a congregational case study is based on the interview questions used with the congregations studied for this book. Added are scales adapted from the pre-existing conditions in chapter 4. These were not used in my interviews for an obvious reason—it was only during the study that these emerged as important factors for responding to resistance.

It is suggested that a team conduct this study. An initial step is for the team to study the text together and then to interview the pastor and as many lay leaders as can be fitted in during a workable time frame. If instances of resistance are cited, it is important to speak with people who have resisted to see if they believe they were listened to. Interviews can be done with individuals or groups. It was helpful in the case studies to have the printed initiative>< resistance diagram (see page 140) and the questions in the hands of those interviewed. As data are collected, the team will want to collate the material and prepare a narrative study to be offered to the congregation.

An added element can be the use of the constructive cycle model presented in this chapter. It is not suggested that this be used in interviews, but it can be a handout when the printed report is presented, and when the team offers its assessment of the ways in which the congregation has lived through the cycle. Leaders should be aware that more than one "cycle" of initiative and resistance can be happening simultaneously. Of particular value is to apply the cycle to particular times when initiatives and resistance have met in the congregation's experience.

Information gleaned from this exercise can be most useful to the congregation's leaders as they plan for the future. I would suggest that they engage in a period of reflection on the team's analysis of how the congregation worked through the cycle. Further, it is suggested that all new leaders be trained in the value and process of the initiative><resistance model. This training should include the core theories presented in this book and particular findings from the case study of the congregation. It is advisable that a case study be done anew at least every two years.

A CONGREGATIONAL CASE STUDY

Interviews will be held with the pastor and staff, and with key lay leaders. To understand the theme of this study, the following diagram will be our starting point:

Figure 12
The initiative ✕ resistance process

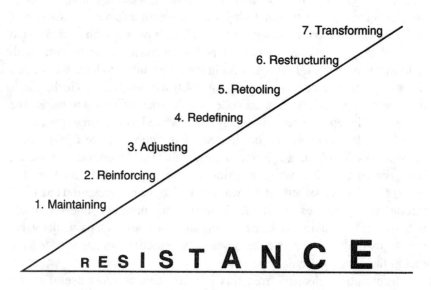

On the slanted matrix the degree of the initiative can be seen. As that On degree increases, as the diagram shows, resistance to change can also grow. The core question is how the pastor and other congregational leaders have learned to approach and deal with resistance.

1. In what situations, ways, and times have the pastor and lay leaders initiated or supported actions that resulted in significant changes in your congregation? Where would you place these changes (1-7) on the continuum?

2. In what ways were you and others prepared for such initiatives (for example, training, prayer, vision presentations, group discussions)?

3. How would you characterize the pastor and other leaders' leadership styles in such times?

4. Are there ways in which the congregation could have been better prepared for these times of change?

5.   Please evaluate the congregation on several scales:
     a. A place where people trust and can be trusted:

         1   2   3   4   5   6   7   8   9   10

         Comments

     b. Leadership is shared by pastor and lay members.

         1   2   3   4   5   6   7   8   9   10

         Comments

     c. The congregation has a vision for the future.

         1   2   3   4   5   6   7   8   9   10

         Comments

d. Spiritual formation is important

1	2	3	4	5	6	7	8	9	10

Comments

e. There is tolerance for change and systems awareness

1	2	3	4	5	6	7	8	9	10

Comments

6. Did any people resist these changes? How did they express their resistance?

7. What was the response of the pastor and lay leaders to this resistance? Did they:

    - Ignore it?

    - Discount it?

    - Acknowledge it?

    - Listen to it?

    - Seek to understand it?

8. Using the resistance-level chart (repeated below), identify instances of resistance in your congregation in as many of the levels as you can. How did leaders respond?

Figure 13
Levels of resistance in congregational life

Resistance	Initiative	Passive/ Active	Range of behavioral responses in resistance	Hoped-for benefits
L1	Maintaining	Passive	Apathy	Valuing an important program
L2	Reinforcing	Passive/ active	Apathy; questioning	Cooperating to strengthen good parts of a congregation's life
L3	Adjusting	Passive & active	Passive disengagement to limited cooperation	Partnership to identify and address needed adjustments
L4	Redefining	Passive & Active	Withdrawing, friendly questioning	Congregation cooperating in craft identity
L5	Retoolng	Passive & active	Loyal opposition, willingness to compromise	Sharing, discerning new forms of action together
L6	Restructuring	Active doubled	Loyal opposition, active disengagement/ "wait it out"	Deep mutual understanding & work to find new directions
L7	Transforming	ACTIVE	Loyal oposition, threatened or real departure	Working, risking, daring to disagree, trust grows

Rules for the Road

As a concluding offering, here are 10 principles that will stand any person who really loves his or her congregation in good stead. Use them in any way you can in the continuing process of making your congregation a healthier place for people to serve God's great mission and ministry in the world that God loves so very much.

1. Resistance is usually healthy, and congregations need to experience resistance to be healthy.

2. When we try to squelch resistance, we threaten the congregation's very existence.

3. Resistance appears when the stability of the congregation is threatened; however, healthy change requires that a system occasionally be destabilized.

4. The congregation's stability needs to be challenged if the congregation is to continue growing and developing. Otherwise, stability produces no more than a deadly status quo.

5. The degree of resistance will intensify as the extent of change increases.

6. If we ignore resistance it may increase, and the congregation will lose members, ideas, and enthusiasm.

7. If resistance is heard respectfully, one payoff may be greater support for the congregation.

8. It is the responsibility of a congregation's clergy and lay leaders to initiate thoughtful changes and to be open to hear the resistance sparked by these change initiatives.

9. Healthy and faithful leaders work openly and welcome others' points of view; they invite expressions of alternatives, for they know that the congregation would be diminished without this dialogue.

10. The give-and-take that comes when change initiators and resisters engage each other openly and with mutual respect can help the congregation be a lively and rich place.

Take these rules and hit the road!

Chapter 1

1. Peter L. Steinke, *Healthy Congregations* (Bethesda, MD: Alban Institute, 1996), 3.

2. Hans Selye, *The Stress of Life*, revised edition (New York: McGraw-Hill), 12.

3. Selye, *Stress of Life*, 13.

4. George Parsons and Speed B. Leas, *Understanding Your Congregation as a System* (Bethesda, MD: Alban Institute, 1993), 7.

5. Parsons and Leas, *Understanding Your Congregation,* 7.

6. Parsons and Leas, *Understanding Your Congregation,* 2.

7. Selye, *Stress of Life,* 37.

8. Roy M. Oswald, Gail D. Hinand, William Chris Hobgood, and Barton M. Lloyd, "The Gap," in *New Visions for the Long Pastorate* (Washington: Alban Institute, 1983), 43-49.

9. Speed Leas and Paul Kittlaus, *Church Fights* (Philadelphia: Westminster, 1973), 28.

Chapter 2

1. Alice Cobble, *Wembi, the Singer of Stories* (St. Louis: Bethany Press, 1960), 48-49 (used with the generous permission of the author).

2. Robert H. Rosen, *Leading People* (New York: Penguin, 1996), 29.

3. Rosen, *Leading People,* 35.

4. Warren Bennis, *On Being a Leader* (Reading, Mass.: Addison-Wesley, 1989), 44.

5. William Chris Hobgood, *The Once and Future Pastor* (Bethesda, MD: Alban Institute, 1998), 69-86.

Chapter 4

1. Lawrence Cada, Raymond Fitz, Gertrude Foley, Thomas Giardino, and Carol Lichtenberg, *Shaping the Coming Age of Religious Life* (New York: Seabury, 1979), 53-61.

2. Mid-Atlantic Training Committee, *Basic Human Relations Training Manual* (Washington: MATC, 1972), 48-51.

3. R. Robert Cueni, *Dinosaur Heart Transplants* (Nashville: Abingdon, 2000), 64.

4. Charles M. Olsen, *Transforming Church Boards* (Bethesda, MD: Alban Institute), 10.

5. Peter L. Steinke, *Healthy Congregations*, 96.

6. Billy Graham, "Choosing Courage," in *The Christian Daily Planner* (Nashville: Thomas Nelson & Sons, 2001).

7. Jay A. Conger, *The Charismatic Leader* (San Francisco: Jossey-Bass, Inc., 1989), 4.

Chapter 5

1. Ronald A. Heifetz, *Leadership Without Easy Answers* (Cambridge, Mass.: Harvard University Press, 1994), 101.

2. Heifetz, *Leadership,* 101.

3. Dudley Weeks, *The Eight Essential Steps to Conflict Resolution* (New York:: Putnam, 1992), 50.

4. Weeks, *Eight Essential Steps*, 50.

5. Weeks, *Eight Essential Steps*, 148.

6. *Thorndike-Barnhart Student Dictionary*, 1988.

7. John C. Harris, *Stress, Power and Ministry* (Washington: Alban Institute, 1977), 3.

8. Jack R. Gibb, *Trust* (Los Angeles: Guild of Tutors Press, 1978), 14.

9. Heifetz, *Leadership*, 101.

10. Jay Conger, *Charismatic Leader,* 32-33.

11. Ethel M. Albert, Theodore C. Denise, and Sheldon P. Peterfruend, *Great Traditions in Ethics* (New York: American Book Company, 1953), 205.

12. MATC, *Training Manual*, 100.

13. Heifetz, *Leadership*, 73-76.

14. Heifetz, *Leadership*, 127.

15. Heifetz, *Leadership,* 74.

16. Heifetz, *Leadership,* 75.

Chapter 6

1. Edwin H. Friedman, *Generation to Generation: Family Process in Church and Synogogue* (New York: Guilford Press, 1985), 35-36.

2. Friedman, *Generation to Generation*, 39.

3. Friedman, *Generation to Generation,*23.

$\mathcal{W}$elcome to the work of Alban Institute...
the leading publisher and congregational resource organization for clergy and laity today.

Your purchase of this book means you have an interest in the kinds of information, research, consulting, networking opportunities and educational seminars that Alban Institute produces and provides. We are a non-denominational, non-profit 25-year-old membership organization dedicated to providing practical and useful support to religious congregations and those who participate in and lead them.

Alban is acknowledged as a pioneer in learning and teaching on *Conflict Management *Faith and Money *Congregational Growth and Change *Leadership Development *Mission and Planning *Clergy Recruitment and Training *Clergy Support, Self-Care and Transition *Spirituality and Faith Development *Congregational Security.

Our membership is comprised of over 8,000 clergy, lay leaders, congregations and institutions who benefit from:
  ❖ *15% discount on hundreds of Alban books*
  ❖ *$50 per-course tuition discount on education seminars*
  ❖ *Subscription to* Congregations, *the Alban journal (a $30 value)*
  ❖ *Access to Alban research and (soon) the "Members-Only" archival section of our web site www.alban.org*

For more information on Alban membership or to be added to our catalog mailing list, call 1-800-486-1318, ext.243 or return this form.

Name and Title: _____

Congregation/Organization: _____

Address: _____

City: _____ Tel.: _____

State: _____ Zip: _____ Email: _____

BKIN

The Alban Institute
Attn: Membership Dept.
7315 Wisconsin Avenue
Suite 1250 West
Bethesda, MD 20814-3211